SANDRA MARIA VAN OPSTAL
SUZANNE STABILE, SERIES EDITOR

FORTY DAYS ON
BEING AN EIGHT

 ENNEAGRAM DAILY REFLECTIONS

ivp

An imprint of InterVarsity Press
Downers Grove, Illinois

InterVarsity Press
P.O. Box 1400, Downers Grove, IL 60515-1426
ivpress.com
email@ivpress.com

InterVarsity Press® is the book-publishing division of InterVarsity Christian Fellowship/USA®, a movement of students and faculty active on campus at hundreds of universities, colleges, and schools of nursing in the United States of America, and a member movement of the International Fellowship of Evangelical Students. For information about local and regional activities, visit intervarsity.org.

All Scripture quotations, unless otherwise indicated, are taken from The Holy Bible, New International Version®, NIV®. Copyright © 1973, 1978, 1984, 2011 by Biblica, Inc.® Used by permission of Zondervan. All rights reserved worldwide. www.zondervan.com. The "NIV" and "New International Version" are trademarks registered in the United States Patent and Trademark Office by Biblica, Inc.™

While any stories in this book are true, some names and identifying information may have been changed to protect the privacy of individuals.

Published in association with the Books & Such Literary Management, 52 Mission Circle, Suite 122, PMB 170, Santa Rosa, CA 95409-5370, www.booksandsuch.com.

Enneagram figure by InterVarsity Press

The publisher cannot verify the accuracy or functionality of website URLs used in this book beyond the date of publication.

Cover design and image composite: David Fassett
Interior design: Daniel van Loon
*Images: gold foil background: © Katsumi Murouchi / Moment Collection / Getty Images
  paper texture background: © Matthieu Tuffet / iStock / Getty Images Plus*

ISBN 978-0-8308-4756-3 (print)
ISBN 978-0-8308-4757-0 (digital)

Printed in the United States of America ♾

Library of Congress Cataloging-in-Publication Data
Names: Van Opstal, Sandra, 1974- author.
Title: Forty days on being an eight / Sandra Maria Van Opstal.
Other titles: 40 days on being an 8
Description: Downers Grove, IL : IVP, [2021] | Series: Enneagram daily reflections
Identifiers: LCCN 2021024326 (print) | LCCN 2021024327 (ebook) | ISBN 9780830847563 (hardcover) | ISBN 9780830847570 (ebook)
Subjects: LCSH: Enneagram. | Personality—Religious aspects—Christianity.
Classification: LCC BF698.35.E54 V36 2021 (print) | LCC BF698.35.E54 (ebook) | DDC 155.2/6—dc23
LC record available at https://lccn.loc.gov/2021024326
LC ebook record available at https://lccn.loc.gov/2021024327

P 20 19 18 17 16 15 14 13 12 11 10 9 8 7 6 5 4 3 2 1
Y 38 37 36 35 34 33 32 31 30 29 28 27 26 25 24 23 22 21

It takes a village to raise a child, but it also takes a community to care for a grown adult. I dedicate this book to the people who have cared for my soul.

To my spiritual director, Marilyn Stewart, who spent decades helping me accept myself with all the cultural nuances of a Latina Eight.

Special thanks to my Enneagram One husband, Karl Ostroski, who created a home where I could be my full self in all of my vulnerability.

WELCOME TO
ENNEAGRAM DAILY REFLECTIONS

Suzanne Stabile

The Enneagram is about nine ways of seeing. The reflections in this series are written from each of those nine ways of seeing. You have a rare opportunity, while reading and thinking about the experiences shared by each author, to expand your understanding of how they see themselves and how they experience others.

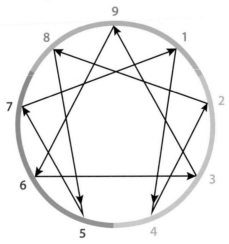

I've committed to teaching the Enneagram, in part, because I believe every person wants at least these two things: to belong, and to live a life that has meaning. And I'm sure that learning and working with the Enneagram has the potential to help all of us with both.

Belonging is complicated. We all want it, but few of us really understand it. The Enneagram identifies—with more accuracy than any other wisdom tool I know—why we can achieve belonging more easily with some people than with others. And it teaches us to find our place in situations and groups without having to displace someone else. (I'm actually convinced that it's the answer to world peace, but some have suggested that I could be exaggerating just a bit.)

If our lives are to have meaning beyond ourselves, we will have to develop the capacity to understand, value, and respect people who see the world differently than we do. We will have to learn to name our own gifts and identify our weaknesses, and the Enneagram reveals both at the same time.

The idea that we are all pretty much alike is shattered by the end of an introductory Enneagram workshop or after reading the last page of a good primer. But for those who are teachable and open to receiving Enneagram wisdom about each of the nine personality types, the shock is accompanied by a beautiful and unexpected gift: they find that they have more compassion for themselves and more grace for others and it's a guarantee.

The authors in this series, representing the nine Enneagram types, have used that compassion to move toward a greater understanding of themselves and others whose lives intersect with theirs in big and small ways. They write from experiences that reflect racial and cultural differences, and they have been influenced by their personal faith commitments. In working with spiritual directors, therapists, and pastors they identified many of their own habits and fears, behaviors and motivations, gifts and challenges. And they courageously talked with those who are close to them about how they are seen and experienced in relationship.

As you begin reading, I think it will be helpful for you to be generous with yourself. Reflect on your own life—where you've been and where you're going. And I hope you will consider the difference between change and transformation. *Change* is when we take on something new. *Transformation* occurs when something old falls away, usually beyond our control. When we see a movie, read a book, or perhaps hear a sermon that we believe "changed our lives," it will seldom, if ever, become transformative. It's a good thing and we may have learned a valuable life lesson, but that's not transformation. Transformation occurs when you have an experience that changes the way you understand life and its mysteries.

When my dad died, I immediately looked for the leather journal I had given to him years before with the request that he fill it with stories and things he wanted me to know. He had only written on one page:

Anything I have achieved or accomplished
in my life is because of the gift of your mother
as my wife. You should get to know her.

I thought I knew her, but I followed his advice, and it was one of the most transformative experiences of my life.

From a place of vulnerability and generosity, each author in this series invites us to walk with them for forty days on their journeys toward transformation. I hope you will not limit your reading to only your number. Read about your spouse or a friend. Consider reading about the type you suspect represents your parents or your siblings. You might even want to read about someone you have little affection for but are willing to try to understand.

You can never change *how* you see, but you can change what you *do* with how you see.

ON BEING AN EIGHT

Fósforito!

The explosion happened so quickly there was no stopping it. My mother used to call me "tiny match" when she saw this fire exploding from me. Words and sounds came out of my mouth that to this day I don't recall. I'm pretty sure there were actual flames coming out from my body.

I could hear my mother's voice telling me to respond *con calma*, but I could not bring myself to pause.

I had just turned thirty and had been seeing my spiritual director, Marilyn Stewart, for a few years. She believed that you should enter the Enneagram journey once two things happened: one, you were mature enough to deal with the patterns of darkness in your life and, two, you had hit a major leadership crisis. These two indicators would most help you find your Enneagram type. This explosion—a confrontation with a colleague—began my Enneagram journey.

Marilyn was a national spiritual director with InterVarsity Christian Fellowship (IVCF), and she and her husband, Doug, trained and offered direction to the team of spiritual directors with IVCF. She was a white Anglican woman who had spent years in ministry in Latin America. For more than a decade Marilyn saw me through ministry transitions, seminary, marriage, miscarriage, infertility, glass ceilings, and the systemic oppression I experienced both as a Latina in evangelicalism and as a pastor in a disenfranchised community.

The day of the explosion, Marilyn smiled, let out a chuckle, and said, "Well, Sandrita, it's time to do some Enneagram work."

The next time I had a three-day retreat scheduled, she sent me off with a journal, my Bible, a watch, and an audio set of lectures on the Enneagram. She said, "Do not guess your type until you have listened all the way through the circle. Do *not* take a test online. Do not ask anyone what they think you are. This is a spiritual pilgrimage."

She talked about the process like it was a sacred rite of passage. Like I was going on a journey to find a mirror that would show me myself for the first time. My whole self. My ugly self. My beautiful self. My dangerous self.

That weekend I listened. I cried when I remembered the pain I had experienced because of certain types' dysfunction and the joy I felt when they were healthy. I laughed when I heard about the antics of other types, as if I could see their behavior in the distance. Then I cried and laughed at the same time—that thing you do when you are simultaneously overjoyed and ashamed. Instead of observing from afar, I felt I was being examined from within. I had found my type.

I am an Eight.

I am an Eight with a strong Seven wing.

I am a Latina Eight.

I am an intuitive feeler Eight.

I am an Eight with a knack for saying the thing everyone thinks.

I cried and thought, *Oh my, that's me*. I laughed and thought, *Yes! That's me*. I had found the mirror that exposed my whole self, and I felt relieved.

Marilyn met me when I had completed the listening process. She was not surprised to learn that I was an Eight, given my passion for justice, relentless truth telling, and, most of all, my intensity and energy level.

Finding your Enneagram type is like finding your superpower—and your kryptonite. I love being an Eight. It worked for me, and it worked for the organizations I led . . . until it didn't. I hit a wall. Like an overused tool, my Eightness became ineffective and I had to relearn some things.

We live in a world where we curate our image. We crop, filter, edit, and enhance ourselves, so that much of what people see is our false self—the person we *want* them to see. Problem is, show someone an angle of yourself long enough and you begin to believe that it's actually you.

The Enneagram journey has been one of seeing myself without filters. Learning to embrace the parts of who I am that are unique.

With increased confidence in God's love for me and God's presence in me, I have been able to confront the wounded parts and broken patterns that need attention. This has meant rejecting the lie that I am too much. Too strong. Too assertive. It has meant paying attention when my gut reacts and then naming my triggers. It has meant accepting that there are not many who can take the blows and choose the risks I do. By accepting God's grace and presence in places of pain, I have been able to admit weakness instead of portraying strength as a way of holding people at a distance.

A guiding passage for freedom in my inner life has been 2 Corinthians 12:9-10:

> [The Lord] said to me, "My grace is sufficient for you, for my power is made perfect in weakness." Therefore I will boast all the more gladly about my weaknesses, so that Christ's power may rest on me. That is why, for Christ's sake, I delight in weaknesses, in insults, in hardships, in persecutions, in difficulties. For when I am weak, then I am strong.

Strength is not found in ignoring the thorns in our flesh. It is not found in pretending we don't feel pain or sadness. It is precisely in our weakness that God's power comes through. It is in that place of grace that I am reminded I can move mountains and start revolutions as long as I am rooted in and fueled by the power of God's Spirit. My ability to admit the need becomes the invitation to receive that power. Thus speaking truth to power from power.

◎ ◎ ◎ ◎

My Enneagram journey as a Latina has been complicated since there are so few Black, indigenous, and people of color (BIPOC) voices represented in the Enneagram world. I've had to use my acquired skills of interpretation and contextualization to arrive at helpful material. We are embodied humans who interpret life from our cultural location. You may not ever hear an author say, "As an affluent and educated white man, I experience . . . ," but the reality is that they're speaking from that location.

Our ethnic, racial, and socioeconomic experiences shape how we interact with God and others. We carry collective cultural values as well as racialized experiences. Therefore there have been many times when I have disagreed with materials that describe the experience of the Eight. I have heard things like, "Eights don't care what others think." If you are an underrepresented, underpaid Latina who comes from a community that values hospitality and you work in an institution where challenging the status quo can cost you your job, you will care what people think.

This is the "Enneagram so white" critique that has kept many BIPOC folks from warming up to the tool. I'm thankful that InterVarsity Press has invited many of us to speak to these realities along the way. I hope it blesses you to consider how your own cultural location affects you.

I pray that you allow yourself the space to name and receive how your collective values and embodied humanity have shaped how you view yourself, God, and the world. Maybe spend a moment even before getting into the devotional to create a list or drawing of all the factors that have shaped you. That can be the first page of your journal as you show up before your Creator.

My prayer is that I do not waste your time. I know how we Eights feel about that. Coming from a communal Latina heritage and having a personality that centers on relationships, I have often found it hard to distinguish the development of self-awareness from narcissism. I thought, *Why spend so much time down a rabbit hole of self-focus and self-actualization when the world is hurting and people are just trying to get their basic needs of safety met?*

But I discovered that by seeing myself and identifying my own longings and laments, I have been able to develop empathy for others. In finding myself, my heart has expanded to love others. We do the work of healing for ourselves so that our healing invites others to their own healing.

Whether you are an Eight, have an Eight wing, or are in a close relationship with an Eight, you are invited on this journey. My hope is that in this daily pause you make for God, you will find more power and rest.

May we love others and rebuild a just world.

STOP. NO, REALLY—STOP

HAS ANYONE EVER SAID you have an exhausting amount of energy? Do they tell you they need a nap after hearing about your schedule? Well, welcome to the life of an Eight! Who has time to think about how exhausted they are? Who has the luxury of taking a nap? There are things to get done and a world to save. We can rest afterward. The problem is that we don't rest!

Rest is salvation for the Eight.

It only took me a decade to figure that out, but I'm finally discovering the sacred rhythms that work for me. In our family we practice a weekly Sabbath, a monthly retreat day, and two three-day silent retreats a year, usually in July and January. These have been a spiritual, mental, and physical salvation.

During one of my January retreats, as I was entering into reflection on my Enneagram number (as I always do), I came across the SNAP concept in the book *The Road Back to You* by Ian Morgan Cron and Suzanne Stabile. SNAP stands for "stop, notice, ask, pivot"—the tools that help us become healthy in our type. When I got to the section on the Eight, I read, "Stop. Literally stop. If possible, put down whatever you are doing. Breathe."

At first, I laughed aloud—a lot—and I almost rolled onto the ground laughing. Then I began to cry—a lot—like I was on the ground on my face because I realized I was so tired. As Eights, we have more energy than any other number, but when we are empty, we hit the wall both physically and emotionally.

Psalm 46:10 says, "Be still, and know that I am God." But for those of us who are driven by the desire to make things right in the world, it is difficult to hear that invitation. If we are going to feel the weight of that truth, we must reflect on the reality of God's strength.

Sometimes I look at the activists, entrepreneurs, and leaders in my circle of friends and notice that many of us have adapted to patterns we never wanted for ourselves. Men in these circles particularly often seem to be disconnected from their need to rest from work. There is always one more phone call, client meeting, student request, or project. Engendered expectations around family and home life give them a pass to continue until physical or relational crisis hits.

I remember a repeated conversation I had with an Asian leader I coached in which I always asked him the same question: "How is your schedule working out for your health and the health of your family?"

I fall into those same patterns, but as a woman, engendered expectations compel me to at least seek balance, even if I don't attain it.

Stop. No, really, truly, stop. Breathe. If you can, still your body and find your center with both feet on the ground. Take a five-second breath in and a five-second breath out. Be still.

What invitation does God have for you today? What truth does God want you to know about the Holy Spirit's work in you and in the world?

THANK YOUR BODY

MOST MORNINGS I take a deep breath, rub my face, plant my feet on the floor, and start moving. As my groggy self makes coffee I give myself a pep talk, telling myself I'm strong and I have it in me to do whatever crazy adventure is on my calendar that day.

By the time I get to the end of my day I'm not really sure what has happened. Some days I feel like a wet rag that's been squeezed out, while other days I'm pretty sure I've been hit by a semi-truck. Somewhere between the start and the end I got slammed by comments, silence, or emotional energy, but I made it through. Problem is, when you stop, you realize what you've just experienced.

It's like the end of that yoga session when your instructor says, "Thank your body for all the hard work it's done today." Suddenly a rush of tears falls as you acknowledge that your body has indeed done a lot of hard work. It survived countless hours of sitting at a desk squeezing out work you didn't think was possible to get done. It lifted children who are getting too old to be picked up but who were waiting for you *all day long*. You stayed present to your partner who was glad to finally have an adult conversation after a day with the kids. It got you through household chores and more, and finally, at the end of the day, you must say thank you.

The invitation today is to thank yourself. It's OK to notice pain. It's human to feel exhaustion. It's your superpower to push through. But some days we just gotta walk in gratitude for the things we were able to accomplish instead of wondering why we couldn't do more.

When we practice gratitude, we can continue to be the self-confident and willful people others depend on to get the job done. When we practice gratitude, we can release ourselves from the need to confront and challenge the situations we weren't invited to change. When we practice gratitude, we invest in our own healing.

Ephesians 2:10 says we are "God's handiwork, created in Christ Jesus to do good works." I remember from studying this passage in New Testament Greek that the word *poiema* (translated "handiwork") gives us our English word "poetry." We are God's poetry. That still stuns me.

We were crafted and designed for good work. Sometimes that work is hard on us, even though it's good. For some of us, that's how we *know* it's good—we feel the wear and tear. Well, then, it's OK that God made us that way. But let's remember to thank God for fashioning us so.

What are the ways the Holy Spirit invites you into self-gratitude?

Review your day. What brought you release? What came at a cost? What was the wear and tear on your body? Thank your body for the hard work it has done today.

GOD GRANTS SLEEP

"IF THERE WAS A CLASS with a grade for sleep, I'm sure you'd figure out how to do it and get an *A*."

My friend's words have stayed with me for over a decade. They were right. They *are* right. I have a hard time sleeping. I lie awake for long periods of time, spinning in my thoughts. When I finally do get to sleep, I wake up repeatedly. I don't feel rested and I certainly never nap.

Who has time for sleep? Certainly not an Eight. Who will get things done? Who will move things forward? Who will save the world? If we stop and sleep, what might happen while we're down?

This self-talk is not conscious, but it's there constantly, below the surface. This is the energy and intensity for which we are applauded and rewarded. This is also secretly the control we assert for fear of being left behind, taken advantage of, or manipulated. We work because we don't want to be caught unprepared for any possible outcome. It's even more heightened if we are involved in service to vulnerable communities that "need" our attention. The work never stops.

We take our concerned, overcaffeinated, underexercised bodies to bed at night and attempt to sleep. But we struggle. Even when we try to make sleep a priority, our minds and bodies are often unable to find release. We have to admit that sleep is difficult when we live as if the weight of the world is on us.

Can I free us a little by sharing some truth? God doesn't need our tired selves to do God's work. Christ is the true advocate. Christ is the one who sustains and advances the work of God's kingdom through the power of the Holy Spirit. God is not trembling when we fall asleep. Scripture orients our disoriented thoughts. Listen to this:

> Unless the LORD builds the house,
>   the builders labor in vain.
> Unless the LORD watches over the city,
>   the guards stand watch in vain.
> In vain you rise early
>   and stay up late,
> toiling for food to eat—
>   for he grants sleep to those he loves.
>   (Psalm 127:1-2)

Did you catch that God is the one who grants sleep? Did you catch that it's because we are loved? We are not on our own. We are not the only ones working. I love this invitation to sleep. I need this invitation to sleep. Thank you, God!

Take a few minutes and review your sleep this week. You may have to guess or you may have a tool that helps you track your sleep. Be honest with yourself.

Is there something keeping you from a night of deep sleep? Is there something you might do to increase your rest? A new bedtime routine? Exercise? Scheduling a time for your last meal? Buying a new pillow? Make a plan to invest in your health.

CHOCOLATE, COMFORT, AND CONTROL

CHOCOLATE! Was that the thing you turned to last night to soothe yourself? Maybe it was whiskey or Cheetos. Maybe it's not even that you ate Cheetos; it's that you consumed the *whole bag* of Cheetos. Perhaps the episodes of eating secretly at night have begun to accumulate. Maybe you're wondering if you have a problem with alcohol. That is a good question for an Eight to ask.

Food is my addiction of choice. I have joined support groups, spoken to a counselor, and prayed for deliverance from my patterns. I am not merely a stress eater; I am compulsively drawn to food and it is difficult to control. That feels embarrassing to say aloud. I remember a time when I was young eating an entire bag of chocolate chips. In college I ate two sleeves of crackers in one sitting. I had to develop a system of identifying "abuse foods" and not allowing them into my presence.

In my adult years I've had lots of friends tease me about my lunchboxes filled with healthy snacks. But I've found that if I snack throughout the day, I'm less likely to go completely overboard. I generally love veggies, meat, fruits, and water. For the most part I am functionally a Paleo-style eater—except for all those carbs and sugars I pop into my mouth.

As Eights, we say to ourselves, "I'll take what I want!" We need more . . . and more . . . and more . . . anything to keep from facing the feelings we don't know how to manage. One more piece, one more episode, one more glass. And the less healthy we are, the less likely we are to realize we're heading down that spiral. We specialize in excess as an antidote to boredom. Just last week I had a night when I stayed up too late, watched too many episodes, and ate too many chips.

We have to stop the madness, and that starts by letting someone in on our dirty little secret. When I fall into the spiral, I confess to a trusted friend that I had another bad night and am headed in the wrong direction. Revealing my weakness is half the battle. Then comes the other part. . . .

Fasting! Fasting is one of the most powerful activities an Eight can engage in because it allows us to stop, cease, abstain—all those words we really don't like. Which is why we like to quote Isaiah 58 so much:

> Is not this the kind of fasting I have chosen:
>> to loose the chains of injustice
>> and untie the cords of the yoke,
> to set the oppressed free
>> and break every yoke? (Isaiah 58:6)

Yes, we Eights believe in justice, but we also want our chocolate. And we don't like to be controlled. No one is gonna tell us when and what to consume. "No limits" is our motto for life, and fasting is literally the opposite of that.

Fasting allows us to be present to our bodies and to name the desires at work in us. Without judging ourselves, we can feel the stress inviting us to indulge in a soothing mechanism and then confront it. It's while fasting that we can receive God's words to us: "I love you just as you are, and I am with you, so you can let go." The practice of fasting invites us to notice how present we are to God and to deepen our faith in God's participation in our lives.

Be honest with yourself and name the things you are turning to in order to decompress.

Choose something that is a trigger for you and abstain just for the day—maybe extend it into a week.

Write down your reflections.

Eat and drink slowly for one of your meals this week and pay attention to the effect it has on you.

DETACHING FROM POWER

DAYS HAD GONE BY without a quiet afternoon when I found myself in a mental sparring match with my toddlers. We stared one another down, refusing to budge. By the time I got to the end of the day, my body was sore from the emotional tug-of-war.

My spouse could not understand why I was so affected by our littles. I probably shouldn't have been, but I experienced their actions as a test of my power. And I don't do well when people test my power, so I was going to remind them that Mama was stronger than they were. Now, looking back, I realize how foolish I was in my approach.

How can a three-year-old possibly have more power than an adult? Clearly they were testing my boundaries. Clearly I was operating out of the fear of being controlled within other relationships and spaces. Sometimes it is another adult—an equal—one-upping us in the workplace or pushing us down in a social situation. Is our response to engage or disengage? Is our instinct to grab hold of power or detach from the desire for it?

If our instinct is to fight back, hit hard, and seize the power in every situation, then we have some work to do. As Eights we don't necessarily need to control others, but we hate it when someone tries to assert control over us. We can find freedom from grasping power by practicing contemplative and patient waiting. We can go against our nature by reminding ourselves that striving for power is not the way. Detaching from power is the way.

I have worked with many Eights, especially men, who regret the times when they have overwhelmed others with their bluntness, scaring them away when that was not their intent, or giving in to impatience when things didn't go well. I'm sure we can all recall occasions when we have offended people with our aggressive style. We know we have to do the work to change.

Two things will help us in this process. The first is slowing down. I know Eights find this very stressful, even a waste of time, but it can be good to detach from the pace that keeps us one step ahead of everyone else. The second is to be intentional about tenderness with loved ones, whether our partner, child, or friend (someone who is human—no pets). This giving of vulnerable emotion will help us release control of relationships in our life.

> Take a day this week to be slow. Drive slowly, eat slowly, and walk slowly. Create space for connection with God, yourself, and others.

ANXIOUS TIMES

ANXIETY WAS NOT SOMETHING I experienced before the Covid-19 pandemic. I felt anxiousness. I experienced stress. I even lost my cool because I felt overwhelmed by the pressures of life and the injustice of the world. What I did not feel was anxiety.

So when anxiety came into my life for the first time, I was completely caught off guard. Eventually I recognized it for what it was and talked with my partner about it. Could it be that even I, a fierce woman, could experience anxiety? Was I that weak? Was I that needy? Was I that broken? In my Eight space I wanted to hide what I was going through, but I couldn't. It was too visible. And eventually, even though Eights are less inclined to seek out therapy or counseling, I knew I needed someone.

As Eights—especially those of us with a Seven wing—we know that others feel the energy we bring into a room. We know we have the power and ability to create atmosphere. We carry that responsibility as we are distinctly designed to carry it. Like an ox who can bear the load because of its strength, we feel the reality of the gift and burden. We get it when we hear the words of Jesus in Luke 9:23: "Whoever wants to be my disciple must deny themselves and take up their cross daily and follow me." We specialize in modeling that for others and inspiring them to do the same.

We live in the reality that struggle results in success.

It is precisely because we carry the load in our families, communities, and churches that we should consider Jesus' invitation seriously. It is in light of the burden we carry that we ought to consider why, how, and for whom we are carrying it. In times of added anxiety, we need to hear some other words from Jesus—invading words—when he invites us (or is it a command?) to "come to me, all you who are weary and burdened, and I will give you rest. Take my yoke upon you and learn from me, for I am gentle and humble in heart, and you will find rest for your souls. For my yoke is easy and my burden is light" (Matthew 11:28-30).

As familiar as those verses are, there is still something in me that always offers up a sigh of relief or a wail of gratitude when I receive the invitation. Like an exhausted child who wants to stay awake and fights off sleep at the end of the day, we fight our Creator who wants to carry the yoke with us. Who wants us to trade the yoke we have fashioned for the yoke God has for us—one that is easy and light when carried with the strength and power of our Creator. This lightness and rest in the midst of weariness invite us to peace in the midst of anxiety because we know we are not in it alone.

Take a moment and lie down on the ground. Put one hand on your heart and one on your belly. Feel the breath as it circulates through your body. What do you notice about yourself? How are you experiencing your body today?

Still lying down, repeat the word *rest*. Now repeat the word *peace*. Note additional ideas circulating in your mind.

Write out the verses of Matthew 11:28-30 in your journal, then jot down words or draw a picture in response to the invitation Jesus has for you today.

NAMASTE

"HELL, NO! I don't want to do yoga!"

"That's gonna be a hard 'no' for me on the yoga."

"Um, yeah, not today—no yoga for me."

I alternate among these three phrases when someone asks me to join them in their yoga practice. I like my exercise to be intense and extreme, with loud music in the background. I want someone yelling at me to kick higher, not someone gently repositioning my rear end. I want to feel like I overcame a mountain, not like I am one. Breathing, patience, and still strength are not for me.

I concede that practices like yoga invite us to pay attention to our bodies—the very thing Eights are so good at ignoring. It's why we can go so long pushing through physical and emotional pain. It's how we get so much done in so little time. It's the reason we can hold our pee long enough to accomplish one more task. It's what makes us like bulls or oxen. But who wants to live like a beast of burden? And so . . . I do try to practice yoga, even though as an Eight I fight it.

Yoga invites us to set an intention. To allow space for our list of choices to scroll before us. To acknowledge, feel, and release pain and fear. To choose what our day will be about. This is all beautiful and terrifying to me as an Eight, because if I allow myself to acknowledge fear and desire, it will expose how vulnerable I really am. The "I am strong" false self will try to shut down the full and true self, which holds onto crushed dreams and insecurities but has no brave space in which to process them.

A yoga session ends with a bow and the spoken word "namaste," which literally means, "I bow to you." It says to the people around you that you see them and honor them. When I learned that, I almost flipped out. Who wants to be seen by someone else?

However, *namaste* carries an intense reminder for people of faith. First, we are created in God's image and we bear God's image. So someone can honor God's presence, which we know lives in us. Second, we are seen by God. When we allow others to see and honor us, we are reminded that God's eyes and God's presence are with us. And last, the practice of making time to recognize and be seen by God and others gives us the courage and humility to honor others and see them.

Take a minute to breathe in and breathe out and sense what you are carrying in your body. Name it and offer it to God. Find time to do this regularly.

Where are the brave spaces in which you can process your feelings? What is the cost of not allowing yourself that space—to yourself and others?

How does it make you feel to know you are seen by God and others? What does that teach you about yourself?

SEXUAL INTIMACY

GROWING UP IN THE purity culture of the early nineties as a woman of color in a white church context was hella confusing. It had me questioning my Latina culture, my body, and my sexual desires. I was made to feel lewd instead of human.

Many of us in those days were taught that our desires were wrong instead of being given tools and categories to address them. Even if we eventually married and finally felt we might be in a safe space, we were so traumatized by the journey we didn't feel free.

Eights enjoy fighting, sex, and adventure as ways to feel connected. The lust of an Eight in all of its expressions is translated into intensity. Eights experience deep joy in their sexuality. Sex is a way of feeling closer to one's partner. We are passionate "go big or go home" people.

I was taught I could not have sex before marriage, which only made me want it more. When I was finally married, I wanted to indulge my passions, but part of me was still affected by those perspectives on my sexuality. Brown and Black women's bodies were (and are still) constantly caricatured and policed by others. I had been told my passion was bad, and now I was just supposed to flip a switch?

The act of sex is not just an exchange of bodies; it is deeply spiritual and personal. As a protective person I want to guard myself from anything that makes me feel seen and known. Sexual intimacy is just that. It invites someone to be close to you. It invites someone to see all of you. It invites exposure of the parts of you that you are ashamed of or insecure about. Who wants this?

Sexual intimacy also invites vulnerability. It lets someone else know you in a way that is private and that can easily be taken advantage of. This is especially hard for those of us who have been harmed, abused, or coerced in our bodies. It is difficult to be available, so we self-protect.

Sex also involves freedom of expression and desire. It means asking your partner for what you want and being clear about what you don't want. Sexual freedom with a partner is difficult when we hold the anger and anxiety of the day in our bodies. The truth is that we want to connect and we want to know we are desired, even with all of our big emotions.

Has *sex* felt like a dirty word to you? Has sexual intimacy been hard for you? Are you protecting yourself from your own sexuality? Do you find yourself asking if you will be rejected?

TOO MUCH

"GOD HAS GIVEN YOU a level of dynamic energy that few around you have."

"You were created with gravitas and the strength to make things happen."

"Your presence can change the atmosphere of a room."

"You can bring people to their feet in applause or their knees in weeping."

"You are inspiring in what you say and how you act."

These are the things we are told by those who love us and are not intimidated by us. This gift of energy Eights have has been given to us for the sake of others, and when we lovingly exercise wisdom in how we wield it, we can create new ways forward.

But there is another set of narratives we encounter as well—especially Eights who are women. They revolve around being "too much."

"You're too bossy."

"Don't get so worked up."

"Your passion is clouding your judgment."

"Why are you so angry?"

"Your voice is too loud."

Take a moment to reject the notion that God made you "too" anything. Eights are the reason things get done in this world. Eights carry the grit of the prophetess Miriam, John the Baptist, and Deborah the judge. We stand in the places no one else is willing to occupy and we say the words that must be spoken. Our leadership helps move people toward new challenges through compelling vision. We should never apologize for our brilliance.

When we do hear those "constructive" words from people, we can do a few things to process them. First, we can consider who's delivering the message. If a close friend has expressed that we are "too much," we might ask ourselves if we were operating only in our gut space or if we were bringing in the harmony of the head and the heart. We are more free to pursue our passion with power when we are tempered by love and thoughtfulness. (I'm not trying to trigger you, I promise. I understand the internal struggle.)

When, in contrast, I receive the "too much" message from someone I don't know, my response is likely to be different. Recently someone responded to a public message I put out in the world with a private message suggesting I had made a "thoughtless" comment. He thought maybe I didn't realize how it sounded, which is why he wanted to tell me in private so he didn't shame me. I assured him my comment was intentional, thoughtful, and compassionate. I didn't know this person and I did not want to spend more energy in his direction.

It's important to process these interactions and your feelings surrounding them with people who create space for you to be your authentic self. Find someone with whom you feel safe to expose your frustrations and insecurities about being told you are "too much." Discuss the experience with them when you have the energy to engage the issue. Allow your heart to be vulnerable and confess that the process is difficult for you because you fear rejection for your big feelings.

> Practice mirror ministry by standing in front of a mirror and listing out loud all the positive, God-given, Creator-breathed gifts that are contained in the body and person you see.

> Read Psalm 139. Breathe in through your nose and out through your mouth a few slow, deep breaths. Inhale: "You have formed me." Exhale: "I am fearfully and wonderfully made."

CURATING YOUR IMAGE

DO YOU EVER FEEL boxed in or disrespected?

When you hear or see a comment that is clearly in reference to you, does it shock you into defense mode? What if the comment is public and you feel both unseen and indignant? Does it take everything in your being not to attack back?

Eights have a strong presence, which often fools people into believing that we have no feelings or are impermeable. But no one is. In those moments I find myself breathing and asking God to allow me to take a moment before responding. In those moments it's not the criticism that hurts but the incorrect analysis that gets made. It's feeling unseen. Feeling misunderstood. Feeling judged. Feeling unknown.

I love Eights, so I tend to surround myself with them. Watching Asian American Eight women speak out is particularly exciting, because people's stereotype of Asian women is that they are deferent. However, it can be incredibly unnerving for these women to operate with their God-given passion for justice and speak up with courage against a cultural expectation. Even if they cuss you out and say they don't care what anyone thinks, there is vulnerability underneath. The reality is that for women, especially women of color, our assertiveness is not often celebrated. This causes us to expend way too much energy on image control.

Men in positions of power who are Eights may not feel the need to curate their image or lighten their response if someone is attacking them, but women are judged by different standards. What is assertive in men is seen as aggressive in women.

Instead of curating ourselves and fixing our image—or posting a scathing response and going on the attack—let's just pause. Not engaging might be the best option. We can trust that our deeds and reputation will speak for themselves. Let's not repay hate with hate.

List some interactions you've had in which you felt someone was asserting social force or control over you. Speak the words "Do not engage" to yourself for one minute on the clock.

How do you feel?

SCARED OF YOU

IMAGINE A SMALL gathering of close friends sharing funny stories about a recent trip they just took. I had this moment recently, and I thought to myself, *Finally. A place where I can be myself and there is no penalty for honesty.*

That thought was interrupted by a comment, one I hear often from polite white folks who eventually call me friend: "Did you know I was scared of you when I met you?"

Yes, of course you were scared of me.

My communication scared you. I came at you direct. I spoke my truth in the rooms where power was threatened. That's what you do when you know there is a better way to live. You say what needs to be heard.

My presence scared you. I am a Latina raised by a fiery Colombiana and an argumentative Argentino. I fill space, with my Seven wing carrying the laughter and the party, and my Eight bearing the whip. Yes, I imagine I do scare you. *Y que?* So what?

But let's be honest. Doesn't it feel better for someone to fear us than disrespect us? If we are real with ourselves, the power we feel when others fear us is more comfortable than the longing we feel for people to like us.

But what if we allowed ourselves the freedom to admit that we are deeply hurt when people are scared of us? What if we acknowledged that it makes us feel we aren't likeable—only tolerable? Why is it so hard to accept that we desire being feared only so we can shelter ourselves from the rejection and disappointment? It's OK.

I saw an Enneagram meme not long ago that showed a picture of a large lion with the caption "Eights on the outside" and a small kitten below with the caption "Eights on the inside." Of course when I saw it I laughed, but it also made me question how people saw me. Was I really scary because I acted like a lioness, or was it others' interpretation of me given my cultural way of expressing myself? Was it their own insecurity or fragility around the topics I advocated for, or was I really being assertive? Was my assertiveness being seen as aggression because I am a woman?

I love lions, tigers, panthers, and other large cats because they are beautiful and dangerous, poised and potent, sought after and feared. The reality is that my fierceness is one of my superpowers. It is, however, hard if the people around you feel like your prey.

The process of figuring out if our behavior is coming from a place of health or stress is an important one because we can't allow others to dictate that for us. Eights, especially female Eights, are incredibly misunderstood because we often move from our gut, and we do it quickly and with precision. Before others can even think, we are standing near them ready to pounce (if needed), and they often feel caught off guard.

I can see where this could be experienced as intimidating, scary, overwhelming, and all the other words that appear when our strength hits other people's uncertainty, fragility, and confusion. But how can we know if it is us or them?

Ultimately, I think we are looking for connection with our brothers and sisters. A journey of healing can help us access our deepest emotions and the truth of our interactions.

What are the issues that have caused you to be forceful or aggressive with others?

Who in your life might have felt like prey at some point in their dealings with you?

Review your interactions with this person and consider how you may have approached the situation with more restraint.

HUMBLE WARRIOR

"HUMBLE YOUR WARRIOR," the yoga instructor said as tears streamed down my cheeks. The combination of bowing and hearing the invitation to actively humble myself made me feel very vulnerable.

Who wants to humble themselves? Does anyone even talk about that anymore in a world where we are constantly on the defense? What is humility?

Yet here I was being invited to practice the posture not of an assertive warrior attentive to battle but of vulnerability, bowed down with my eyes not on the world around me or myself but on the ground.

"Humble your warrior."

As a leader, I internalize the message that strength is the only way to lead. As an activist, I am taught that agitation wins. As a human being, I push myself until I experience the limitations of my body. As a fighter, when someone attacks my intentions or my character, the logical thing is to strike back to defend myself.

"Humble your warrior."

Humility invites surrender and openness to God and God's Spirit.

Humility invites self-reflection and honesty about oneself.

Humility invites emptying the self and centering on those most vulnerable.

Humility invites repentance in keeping with tangible change.

Humility results in freedom.

Let Jesus invite you to humble your warrior. According to our King, the way up is down. Even when it is painful.

"Those who exalt themselves will be humbled, and those who humble themselves will be exalted" (Matthew 23:12).

Take Humble Warrior pose. (With your feet in wide stance, step forward with your right leg and bend your knee ninety degrees. Clasp your hands behind your back. Fold your body forward, bringing your torso inside your front leg, and look down at the ground. Lift your arms up and overhead. Hold the pose and take slow, deep breaths.)

While in this pose, hear Jesus' invitation to you: "Humble your warrior."

Say it aloud to yourself and your soul: "Humble your warrior."

Say, "Those who humble themselves will be exalted."

DISTRACTION OR DEPENDENCY

EVER HAD A DAY when you checked your social media account every three minutes? Maybe that day is today. You continue to see the notice that you're "all caught up," but you start searching, and then fifteen minutes later you're in a maze of not only checking content but also comparing your social media engagement to others'. And then you realize your distraction isn't actually a distraction at all—it's a dependency.

We know that social media has major psychological effects on the brain. We can even find ourselves experiencing cravings like someone with a substance addiction. When we post content and are rewarded with likes, shares, and other positive feedback, the brain releases dopamine, which rewards the behavior and perpetuates the cycle. A variety of studies have shown that the average person in the United States touches their phone about 2,600 times a day and spends two to four hours using it.

As an Eight I have found it critical to be aware of the things in my life that are addictive and understand why they offer me a sense of control or power. Whatever Eights do we do with the full force of who we are, so I think it's appropriate to keep an eye on things that can become addictions and excavate why we are so dependent on them. This allows us to be honest about what our behaviors are telling us about our health.

When we find ourselves reaching for the next hit, what is it we're longing for? Is it a boost of affirmation we need? Is it a dose of power we seek? Is it a sense of influence we want to make sure we maintain? Or is this addiction simply a way to escape a reality we need to deal with? We may need some help understanding why we've moved from distraction to dependency. Starting a conversation on the topic with a trusted friend or therapist can be a great part of the process.

God's Spirit is able to search our hearts and help us find liberation. This is the gift of truth the Lord offers us through the prophet Jeremiah:

> The heart is deceitful above all things
>> and beyond cure.
>> Who can understand it?

> "I the LORD search the heart
>> and examine the mind,
> to reward each person according to their conduct,
>> according to what their deeds deserve."
>>> (Jeremiah 17:9-10)

We need a community of people to keep us honest with ourselves and with others. Our hearts will make things up. Our minds will interpret situations in the way that most benefits us. I have been hearing that verse as a warning my whole life, and I used to blow it off. But even those in the mental health professions encourage us to have people with whom we process and confide so we don't downward-spiral into narcissism and dependency.

When I consider the things that distract me and often become dependencies, they involve others' achievements and success, a desire for influence, and a longing to see the world change. In small doses they produce energy and passion, but left unattended they produce distorted drive.

What does it mean that God searches the heart and examines the mind but rewards according to deeds and conduct?

Who are your people? Who are the ones that can keep a loving, trusting eye on how your whole person is doing?

ROOTED IN RIGHTEOUSNESS

TRANSFORMATION TAKES TIME. In many cultures the symbol of wisdom is a large tree. The willow, the oak, the majestic redwood are each praised for their strength, which comes with rootedness as the years go by. In Isaiah 61:3 we are given an image of oaks rooted in righteousness for the display of God's splendor. This ultimate expression of being rooted comes only after the process of transformation. It is only over time as we are rooted in righteousness that we fully live into the impact we can have on the lives of others.

Robert Mulholland in *Invitation to a Journey* defines spiritual formation as the "process of being conformed to the image of Christ for the sake of others." This deepening relationship is central, flowing from wells of intimacy, rest, and connection with God. We take in new information and create space to decide how we might live in response individually and in community.

As an Eight, I have encountered injustices in my community and expectations on the part of others to "do something" that prompted me to carry responsibilities and challenges prematurely, before I had attained enough growth. I see this often in younger leaders who are Eights. In one community I saw an Eight leader called on to lead initiatives he was unprepared for. He didn't ask for help, and when help was offered he declined it. When deadlines arrived he had not completed his work, and it was clear he did not have the resources he needed. He might have felt that accepting help was a sign of weakness. The pattern continued and he never addressed the reasons he was unable to ask for help.

We simply seem compelled to do the work. And, honestly, Eights who are good with words may give the impression that we know what we're doing. We may even get applauded for our words and ideas, but sometimes it's the quietest people who have the most integrated lives. They volunteer, connect with officials, and invest significant resources toward the work of compassion and justice. They know that spiritual formation is a journey toward integrity, a daily discipleship of ordering the mundane in one's life around love for God and neighbor.

So focus on learning from the people you know who are grounded. Listen to the ones who have been doing this work for decades and who have gone through the process of maturing and healing. Remind yourself that all the things you've done up to here in your leadership, every step of the way, every time you said "yes," every time you failed—those are all pieces of the journey. They were training you for where you're at today.

As Eights, we want to be different. We want our world to be different. But rootedness takes time.

Draw an image of a large tree and its roots. Take time to write out brief descriptions of the disciplines or experiences that have rooted you. Thank God that there is work others can't see that is still being done. Ask God to show you that work in your life. What do you want and what do you fear?

ANGER IS DRIVING

"I'M NOT ANGRY; I'M HURT."

I often find myself having to interpret my emotions when I see how my actions are coming across. When I notice people's eyebrows lifting or their bodies leaning backward, it's clear that some interpretation is needed. It can be as simple as "Some Latinas are more demonstrative than other cultures," or a reminder that my passion is not anger. Some days it's a realization that I am indeed communicating anger when that's not what I am feeling at all.

It's important for me to recognize when my negative emotions are filtered through anger. Anger is the driving emotion when I'm going through something difficult. When my friend stops talking to me and I can't figure out why—anger. When someone I've invested in ghosts me—anger. When I can't take it anymore and I've had enough, or when I am beating myself up and feel guilt for not having done enough, people sense my anger. When I feel exposed in a moment where I feel shame for being too much, I retaliate with anger.

It's also important for me to recognize when anger is the appropriate human response. Anger is not bad. It's a way we connect as image bearers of God. God gets angry. Jesus expressed anger. Those of us raised in cultures where it was inappropriate to express anger may feel shut down (which just makes us angrier). We may even have to uncover layers of repressed feelings later in adulthood. If our church setting taught that anger was ungodly or unbiblical, that's even worse. The discipline of connecting our anger to God's righteous anger requires tools many of us were not given, leading many of us to feel as if we are broken, intense, or ungodly.

Anger is an appropriate response to injustice and idolatry. As Eights, we long for and dream toward a world in which all things are made whole as the Lord promises in Revelation 21. This fire for justice is ignited when we are confronted with the wrongness of the world. It's what makes us the brave, courageous people who will do and say what is required, and it's also what gets us in trouble.

In Luke 9, two disciples ask Jesus if they should annihilate a Samaritan village. The disciples might have felt upset that the villagers would not house them and saw that as a huge disrespect to Jesus. They may have been upset that the Samaritans shamed them for going to Jerusalem. We know from many places in Scripture about the animosity of Jews toward Samaritans, so maybe they were upset because as Jews they couldn't believe those half-breeds (yes, I said that—it's how the Jewish people viewed the Samaritans) were rejecting them. What is clear is that the situation angered them to the point of asking Jesus if he wanted them to destroy an entire village. Did you catch that? Children and animals too!

There are many times I have been just as angry as James and John in this story. I am thankful for people who have kept me from my fire-breathing ways, and I have always committed to being that for others.

I can spot a blaze about to ignite in another Eight. I can think of countless times when I had to have a car, hallway, or *cafecito* conversation with someone that went something like this: "You are right to be angry. You are justified in feeling this way given the wrong behavior or attitude that person has. I am not here to try to alter your feelings or perspectives. But I want to catch you before you respond because you *will* burn bridges if you choose the 'aim, fire, ready' approach. Take a minute to allow reflection and love to guide your response. Your anger when submitted to God can be a tool to make things happen. Good things. Godly things."

Martin Luther King Jr. said it like this: "The supreme task is to organize and unite people so that their anger becomes a transforming force."

What tools do you use to identify the source of your anger?

What are the other emotions you feel that appear to be anger, but could use some interpreting?

SUPER STRENGTH

STRENGTH CAN BE ALARMING to people. Strength can trigger negative reactions, including insecurity, fear, and anxiousness. The presence of energy and grit can also be incredibly attractive to people who long for and are mobilized by intensity. Being strong can be a pro or con depending on how one wields their strength in relationship to others.

As an Eight I've learned to be careful with my strength—mostly because I've been told that if I'm not I can harm people. I was given a talk very similar to the one given to Rogue from the X-Men or Elsa from *Frozen*. I've spent much of my leadership with imaginary "gloves" on so my God-given potent energy would not kill or freeze someone. My self-talk was so bad that I told my therapist most people were afraid to get too close to me for fear of getting hurt. The narrative I carry is that people would rather I not be around but they tolerate me because I get things done.

While I think there is a need for thoughtful compassion when wielding the superpowers with which the Holy Spirit has gifted us, it is suffocating to constantly be afraid to hurt someone. It's also exhausting. How can we be free to be fully Eight without doing damage? Increasing our emotional intelligence, which includes both self-awareness and empathy, helps.

It is not just my Eightness or my individual personality that makes me an intense person. The key to my freedom is identifying why God created me and allowed me to experience a particular family and people and culture, as well as the distinctive way he wants to work through my intended design and journey. It has been both my collective narrative and my distinctiveness that led to freedom.

I was shaped by a culture of people who are naturally intense. On my mother's Colombian side I was encouraged to be a physically demonstrative person who communicated with strong positive language and an extra dose of sugar. On my father's Argentine side I was trained to be a decisive communicator who could challenge ideas and be suspicious of easy answers. Both South American cultures were equally demonstrative but in opposite directions. In addition, both of my parents grew up in generations and social-political realities that required grit. If courage was not natural, it was learned through risk-taking. Hope was cultivated through belief and waiting on God.

Paul says to the early church, "Now the Lord is the Spirit, and where the Spirit of the Lord is, there is freedom. And we all, who with unveiled faces contemplate the Lord's glory, are being transformed into his image with ever-increasing glory, which comes from the Lord, who is the Spirit" (2 Corinthians 3:17-18).

Have cultural norms affected your ability to freely live into your God-given design?

What might freedom require on your journey of transformation?

Thank God for both your distinctiveness and your collective identity.

GRIT WITH GRACE

AS AN EIGHT WHO IS an intuitive feeler, I can be extremely demonstrative, but when it comes to my passion for seeing people be right before God, it is not a show.

Jeremiah is a biblical character who connects with the soul of an Eight. He is called the weeping prophet, and he shows us what it's like to bring God's heart into the room. In the middle of his work we hear Jeremiah processing this call:

> To whom can I speak and give warning?
>   Who will listen to me?
> Their ears are closed
>   so they cannot hear.
> The word of the LORD is offensive to them;
>   they find no pleasure in it.
> But I am full of the wrath of the LORD,
>   and I cannot hold it in. (Jeremiah 6:10-11)

This is the feeling many of us have when we are trying to move people. When no one seems to want to listen, we can get real hardass and start to yell even louder, sometimes with little compassion, because the end justifies the means.

We feel like Jeremiah—so consumed with the wrath of God we unleash it on others. While sometimes that move is Spirit-inspired, as it was for Jeremiah, at other times we must consider that our dynamic power exists for the sake of others—even those who are making the harmful decisions. Wise and loving ways of expressing our energy create new ways forward not only for us but for others.

In those moments it has been crucial for me to give myself the space to ask myself a series of questions:

What does my heart feel?
What does my mind think?
What does my gut sense?

This time of reflection allows me to go to a place of inviting joy, peace, patience, slowness, kindness, and compassion into the places where I felt anger, fear, and pride.

The truth is that Jesus is the one who protects, redeems, and rescues the world. I am not. We are not. It is not our job to force things to happen out of anger or a desire for rightness.

What is the invitation you have in your workplace or your community that you feel no one will hear? Speak or write it out and invite God's Spirit to remind you of God's presence.

Are there ways we try to move people with "wrath" (a.k.a. truth telling) that lacks compassion or care? Write down a few times where you have employed creative ways.

BOBCAT

WHEN WE RECENTLY redid the grass in our backyard, a crew had to come in with a Bobcat excavator and pull up what looked, to the untrained eye, like mostly good grass. Over the course of two sweat-drenched days they filled an entire construction dumpster full of concrete, debris, and grass. This was using a Bobcat—what would the job have been like without it? Impossible. The next day the crew laid down thousands of pounds of new dirt and rolled out the grass in just a few hours.

Eights carry the kind of leadership and grit that overcomes denial and pushback from people who are satisfied with the status quo. Eights are the Bobcats of life.

The biblical prophet Jeremiah knew a little about the work of a Bobcat. Although biblical prophets came with a message of freedom, they were seen as disruptors of the status quo. Jeremiah called out the things God placed on his heart. He is known as the weeping prophet because he carried the hope and lament of God. The burden of standing in the tension between what will be and what actually is would cause any of us to weep.

Jeremiah's message was above all one of renewal, but renewal is preceded by a radical removal of the toxic things that exist in our lives. We could call it repentance. Prophets carry with them the heart of God in both challenge and compassion.

In God's call to Jeremiah he says, "I have put my words in your mouth. See, today I appoint you over nations and kingdoms to uproot and tear down, to destroy and overthrow, to build and to plant" (Jeremiah 1:9-10). This call includes three pairs of verbs, the first being "uproot" and "tear down," both of which involve removal. The second set is "destroy" and "overthrow"—again, both removal. It is only the last set that are positive: "build" and "plant." Not only is there a lot of deconstruction going on, the imagery makes sure we understand the totality of it.

The call to risk danger and to influence people, the need for grit in the next step of life, are all attractive to an Eight. This is not because we like pain but because we know we are built for it.

In many spaces in our lives we may feel like we are doing the heavy lifting of digging out a dumpster full of debris to clear a space where real grass can grow. We long to see safe backyards that are constructed well. We Eights are the ones who build with Bobcat leadership. Whether our strength is external or flows from internal resolve, there are few who can match it—we are created for the job. As the Lord assured Jeremiah, God says to us, "Do not be afraid of them, for I am with you and I will rescue you." The ability to sustain that work comes from knowing that God is with us.

What are the things God is inviting you to remove from this world? Places that need demolition? What maintenance do you need to do for sustainability?

What do you dream and imagine could be built once those things are gone?

CALM IN THE STORM

WHEN THE WAVES of uncertainty are crashing.

When the winds of violence are blowing.

When the weight of poverty and oppression are causing us to sink.

How we manage our souls in the middle of the storm is important. Because Eights experience life in the storm.

I remember the story I learned in kids' church of the disciples out in a violent storm and Jesus just sleeping through it. Even thinking of it makes me anxious. I hear the disciples' vulnerability in the question they ask Jesus: "Teacher, don't you care if we drown?" (Mark 4:38). They lack the ability to control the storm that is raging around them. They can't do anything to stop the imminent danger.

That is how I feel when I see the brokenness in the world. I feel small. I have spent decades trying to make a dent, and yet the violence is still crashing all around me. I feel anxious.

Many of us have felt like the disciples on the boat in the storm. Jesus is there. We are arm's length from him. Closer, even. We know Jesus can do something, and we are crying out, "Don't you care if we drown?" In Scripture, God's people experienced slavery, exile, famine, wilderness, and persecution, and they cried out to God in the middle of the crisis, "Don't you care if we drown?"

As a daughter of immigrants and an activist in an urban community, I am well-acquainted with systemic abuse and collective grief. I have done everything in my power to seek justice and speak truth. Communities of color have been crying out at every turn, every crisis. We understand that those in power create policy that impacts all sorts of life-and-death situations, especially in marginalized communities. We're doing what we can to stop the storm from devouring our existence.

Shootings of black men . . . "Don't you care if we drown?"

Child separations and family detention . . . "Don't you care if we drown?"

Native lands commodified . . . "Don't you care if we drown?"

Xenophobic anti-Asian acts . . . "Don't you care if we drown?"

The pandemic's disproportionate effect on Brown and Black communities . . . "Don't you care if we drown?"

Incarcerated friends dying of Covid-19 . . . "Don't you care if we drown?"

The earth's climate changing . . . "Don't you care if we drown?"

We are not at the end of the story. We are still in the middle of the storm, feeling small, feeling anxious, singing as in the chorus of the song "Wake Up, Jesus," from The Porter's Gate: "Jesus, when you gonna wake up?" Later the song asks, "How can you sleep when we're in need?" It ends with the call, "Won't you rise up?"

When God's people were in the midst of slavery, exile, famine, wilderness, and persecution, Jesus did see and he did hear.

He sent us.

Think about a circumstance in which you feel despair and a desire to take things into your own hands. Read Mark 4:35-41, which describes the storm that rose up when the disciples were in a boat at sea. Imagine yourself there. Now picture this: Jesus "got up, rebuked the wind and said to the waves, 'Quiet! Be still!'" (Mark 4:39).

Receive that image of power as you confront the day.

BREAKDOWNS ARE OK

WHEN I WAS A YOUNG GIRL my parents owned an orange VW Beetle. It was a super-cute seventies car, but it constantly broke down, and that was super-infuriating. My parents chose to raise us in an up-and-coming affluent suburb where everyone had a couple of new cars. We, on the other hand, had a Bug. A broken Bug.

It embarrassed us when it made noise in front of the school or got stuck in the middle of a busy intersection. It was also dangerous—one winter we broke down in below-freezing temperatures and I was young and unprepared to walk the few miles home with my parents.

Breakdowns are embarrassing, and the ones that bring the most shame to my Eight sensibilities are my own. Who in the world wants to emotionally crash in front of anyone? Especially when it seems that all the adults in our lives seem to have it together? When our fellow "gut space" folks are strong and self-contained? Why does everyone have to come off so cool?

Isn't that the lie, though? It says that even in our brokenness we need to be polished and sanitized before we can interact with others.

Breakdowns are inevitable when we're running at the speed and intensity of "gut space." Our stressed selves will eventually break. We will come to the point where our striving and our pushing through will fail us. When it happens and we get stuck in the middle of an intersection, what will we do to get out of it? We may want to get out of the car and scream, curse, and stomp around, but that will not solve it. How do we recover?

We are to wait. We are to hope. We are to anticipate God. Isaiah spends time reminding us of God's personhood and promises. He asks us, "Do you not know? Have you not heard?" He then goes on to describe all the things that are true about God:

> The LORD is the everlasting God,
>   the Creator of the ends of the earth.
> He will not grow tired or weary,
>   and his understanding no one can fathom.
> He gives strength to the weary
>   and increases the power of the weak.
> Even youths grow tired and weary,
>   and young men stumble and fall;
> but those who hope in the LORD
>   will renew their strength.
> They will soar on wings like eagles;
>   they will run and not grow weary,
>   they will walk and not be faint. (Isaiah 40:28-31)

In this description we find the power and presence of a Creator who sustains creation and restores the things that are broken. In this description we are reminded that no one can teach God about compassion and justice. No one can add to God's love or healing. No one can restore and renew in the way the everlasting God can. The invitation given to us when we break down is to fall down in the way of a Pentecostal revival . . . to just lay ourselves down in the presence of the Spirit.

When we wait in hopeful anticipation, we acknowledge that we cannot strive our way back to healing. We can't push our way to restoration. We can offer ourselves to the powerful presence of God and allow restoration to begin.

What are you accustomed to doing when you break down? After you scream, curse, and stomp, where do you go?

Take a moment and listen to Isaiah 40 (most Bible apps include an audio feature). Allow the description of God to penetrate the places in your body and soul that are broken down. Admit them—no judgment. Receive the care, love, and protection God wants to offer under God's wings.

FROM THE MOUTH
OF AN ASS

SPEAKING TRUTH TO POWER is not an easy thing to do, so as an Eight I often find myself being called upon or volunteered. This is something I enjoy about being an Eight: people know we are courageous, straightforward, and honest and will uphold just causes.

A number of years ago I was the youngest person to speak at an event and the only woman in the series of talks. The other speakers were decades my senior and held higher-ranking positions. I remember being a combination of nervous, excited, and grateful. I had prepared my words and submitted them in advance. I had practiced with a speaking mentor, and I had prayerfully written out the stories, Scriptures, and exhortations I wanted to offer. God had a word for the community—I was sure of it.

During a prayer time leading up to the event, one friend prayed for me, and all I remember him saying is, "Lord, you choose to speak through anyone you desire. Help us to be available. If you can speak through the mouth of an ass, you can speak through our sister." I didn't know whether to be upset or laugh.

As I preached, I experienced a rush of energy and freedom I had rarely felt before. As I heard the responses from the verbal members of the audience of a few hundred, I sensed that God had prepared me for this moment. It was the clearest sense of partnership with the Holy Spirit I have had to this day.

When I was finished, dozens of people who identified with the message I had given came up to speak with me. Specifically, I remember the matriarch of one of the ethnic communities coming to me and expressing that I had the courage to say what many were thinking.

I knew some were uncomfortable with the topics I addressed and the confidence with which I addressed them. Apparently I had disturbed some people in power and there were rumblings and gatherings, and eventually I received a call asking me to apologize for what I had said. It was a mess.

Only a decade later did I realize that the reference to the story of Balaam's ass in Numbers 22 was perfect. The ass did speak, but only after Balaam—who had power over her—beat her three times. The ass was protecting Balaam, but his response was to beat her for making him seem foolish. That was the treatment I received. God spoke through me, and instead of listening to the warning, those in power were focused on looking foolish and decided to punish me for speaking truth.

After that incident, I asked not to be invited to any more events with that group. I didn't need the headache. But that experience almost two decades ago taught me to speak up, be wise, and expect opposition. It prepared me for the future.

What things have happened in your life to prepare you for leadership?

What "beatings" have you endured?

Thank God for the courage to do what few people would risk doing.

NEVER SEEN IT BEFORE

ONE NOVEMBER EVENING, when I was surrounded by young women of color and daughters of immigrant families, I heard newly elected Vice President Kamala Harris speak these words of life: "While I may be the first woman in this office, I will not be the last. Because every little girl watching tonight sees that this is a country of possibilities. And to the children of our country, regardless of your gender, our country has sent you a clear message: dream with ambition, lead with conviction, and see yourselves in a way that others may not simply because they've never seen it before. But know that we will applaud you every step of the way."

It was an amazing moment of firsts: the first woman, the first woman of color, the first Black, the first Jamaican, the first Asian, the first Indian, and the first daughter of immigrants to be vice president of the United States. It was like we were experiencing our dignity restored and being given the freedom to dream again for those children in the room. It was an opportunity for me to reflect on what my leadership would have looked like if I had seen that as a young girl!

This historical moment changed the narrative for our nation, and we will likely not see the true impact for decades. The presence of women leaders can especially influence how young girls see themselves. Even in the context of the church, research shows that women who attend a church with female clergy enjoy higher levels of self-esteem as adults. Kamala Harris's election victory fed my soul as an Eight, because it helped me imagine a new future for women of color who are economically and vocationally marginalized.

Eights live life to change the narrative and make an impact on the world around them. We are powerful, passionate revolutionaries who thrive in imagining a new way forward. We focus our boundless energies on finding a better way to live. We are wired to be the first and the only. We are gifted to model something that has never been seen before. This day gave me the faith to believe that when we chase justice, we can win.

Eights are crucial for the social imagination of the people around us. Our resourcefulness means we help inspire, model, and mobilize others to live well. We work to make the future just. We carry in our bones the words of Martin Luther King Jr.: "There comes a time when one must take a position that is neither safe, nor politic, nor popular, but he must take it because conscience tells him it is right."

God's Word has given me fuel to dare the impossible and to understand that we are designed to live with intention and given power and grace to do what God has given us to do. Even when people think it's impossible because they have never seen it before.

> And God raised us up with Christ and seated us with him in the heavenly realms in Christ Jesus, in order that in the coming ages he might show the incomparable riches of his grace, expressed in his kindness to us in Christ Jesus. For it is by grace you have been saved, through faith—and this is not from yourselves, it is the gift of God—not by works, so that no one can boast. For we are God's handiwork, created in Christ Jesus to do good works, which God prepared in advance for us to do. (Ephesians 2:6-10)

Allow yourself to dream about the next twelve months. What did God prepare in advance for you? What has someone in your sphere never seen before that you know you can lead others in?

Pray as you take deep breaths. Inhale: "Not my will." Exhale: "But yours be done."

SPIRITUAL DISCIPLINE OF GRIPING

JUST BECAUSE GOD REIGNS doesn't mean empires aren't at work. As people of faith we can often be overwhelmed by the tension between what we know the world ought to be and the reality of what it actually is. As Eights we are wired to deeply empathize with people experiencing injustice around us and seek to alter this reality. We are the kind of people who are unafraid to take a stand on behalf of those unable to defend themselves. We find ourselves wanting to believe that the kingdom is here because our faith tells us it is, but we feel the ache that it is also *coming*.

Our complaints, our crying out, and our admission of anxiety are all biblical responses. Our fear is not the absence of faith. It points to an authentic relationship with the one who knows us and created us. Our exhaustion is not weakness; it's awareness that on this side of the revolution our bodies are limited. And in times of stress, we have to remember not to attack or isolate.

We can gripe to God! Biblical lament allows relief for all of us, but especially those of us who operate in a gut space. Whether this lament comes in written form, poetically crafted, or in the groanings of an ugly cry during our devotional time or nature walk, it is cathartic. Lament releases the tension we feel. This kind of lament is not only acceptable; it is modeled in the Psalms, Lamentations, and the Prophets. It is found in the weeping of King Jesus himself.

We often allow people to silence us. We give them permission to shut down our expressions of fear, exhaustion, and sorrow. Those of us who are Black, indigenous, and people of color need to wail even louder as a way of helping us understand the generational and collective trauma and pain we are experiencing. Denial and lack of self-awareness are not fruits of the Spirit.

It's been important to me not to rush hope. And hope is not the same as a positive attitude (which is a good thing for an Eight like me, who has about nine corrective comments for every one positive remark). Hope is living in light of God's goodness in the midst of God's silence. Social justice scholar Cornel West, in a 2018 interview with Judith Hertog in *The Sun*, says, "Hope is not a mood; it's a virtue. We have a right to be in as dark a mood as we want, because things are indeed bleak. But hope is a virtue—which is to say, it's an excellence that we aspire to. No matter how dark your mood is, you still have a responsibility to aspire to the virtuous. Hope is the refusal to succumb to despair and nihilism."

We can and should share God's Word and celebrate things that are true about our faith. We believe that Jesus is King. We know that this is God's kingdom and Jesus will return to restore and renew all things (Revelation 21). We can and will hang on to hope in the midst of tension because we know that giving in to despair empowers those who are determined to stop us.

What lament have you not let out? What release is your soul asking for this day?

Find the song "How Much Longer?" by Art Hooker, Ben Hardesty, and Courtney Orlando on YouTube. Listen to how it expresses the longing of our hearts: "In the silence, tell me, can you hear the voices calling out of the disappeared? Broken spirits, dormant dreams . . . how much longer will justice sleep?"

IN BETWEEN BATTLES

LIVING OUT OUR FAITH as Eights will often lead us to disrupt the status quo or even get caught up in civil disobedience. Our clear ideas about what is right and wrong will lead us to confront powers that seek to maintain systems and environments that silence and marginalize vulnerable people. As Eights we may find ourselves in battles over issues where integrity is at stake. The hardest part is when we take risks out of concern for others and receive no appreciation for it or partnership in it.

The story of Elijah at Mount Sinai in 1 Kings 19 has been a potent example for me of an embodied Eight experience. Elijah runs away after a victory in battle because his enemies are coming after him. He asks the Lord to take his life, which could be because depression often follows an uplifting experience. But God knows what he needs.

After Elijah has been asleep for a while, an angel wakes him and asks him to eat, drink, and sleep. This repeats itself. Then Elijah spends a "time-out" of forty days in the desert on his way to seek God. When he arrives at the mountain,

God asks him why he is there. Elijah replies, "LORD God All-Powerful, I have always served you the best I can, but the Israelites have broken their agreement with you. They destroyed your altars and killed your prophets. I am the only prophet left alive, and now they are trying to kill me!" (1 Kings 19:10 ERV).

I relate to Elijah's very Eight feeling. Sometimes I too get high blood pressure when people don't obey the rules or when things don't go right. Elijah has hit a threshold with others' incompetence. He is protecting himself and running to God for help. The Lord tells him to stand in front of the mountain and he will pass. There is a windstorm, an earthquake, and a fire. Then the Lord shows up in a "quiet, gentle voice" (1 Kings 19:12 ERV) asking for a second time why he is there. Elijah repeats the same message. His discouraged state of mind remains unchanged even after the assurance of divine presence; his response to God's question has not changed.

Elijah needs to pause in order to see things correctly. The three days of sleeping and nourishment, as well as the forty-day time-out, have allowed him the space he needs to know and name his protest. He may not have the right answers, but at least he has *some* answers. He knows how he feels and is able to express it in the presence of his Lord. Given the space and time, we can all move beyond simply feeling overwhelmed and tired to knowing exactly what we feel. In his case, Elijah was alone, afraid, and hopeless.

I have felt like I needed three days of sleeping and forty days in solitude. I have felt lonely. I have felt hopeless. Leaders and prophets have a hard-ass job and few people understand the weight of an Elijah burden. But as Eights we must get rest, make space to reflect, and listen for God. God will reassure us that we are not alone.

Make a plan to retreat. Only when you settle your mind and rest can you hear God's gentle, quiet voice.

START WASTING TIME

ONE EVENING WHEN I was about to head to bed, my partner was teasing me about not doing anything fun. It went something like this, "Everything you do is serious. You barely ever read fiction, and even when you do it's about gang life and injustice in the inner city or set during a genocide or pandemic. The next time we go on vacation I want you to pick a fiction book with unicorns, dragons, or lasers. You need to rest your brain."

I quickly shot back, "Dragons are a waste of time."

He laughed so hard he doubled onto the floor and almost wet his pants. He just laughed and laughed. During his laughter I went from angry to embarrassed to relieved. My partner was able to see something about me that I could not and call it out. This was both helpful and it exposed me—and I don't like to be exposed.

But he continued, "Reading is a waste of time. Resting is a waste of time. Fun? Waste of time. Laughing? Waste of time. Smooching? Waste of time." He went on and on until I could hardly breathe from my own laughter.

He was right. Unless something had a purpose, I saw it as a "waste of time." I had to admit that I had some serious issues. This was when I was just becoming aware of my Eight-level intensity and my tendency to constantly fight the world.

In my eyes, even vacations are a time to learn and engage the ethnic and historical realities of the places we visit. As my partner recently reminded me, on our honeymoon I constantly asked the staff at the hotel questions about their working conditions. And recently while speaking I talked about the necklace I was wearing—it was from Kenya and I connected it to a need to listen to the voices of the majority world. My friend came up afterward and said, "Even your jewelry has a purpose." I heard it as a compliment, but as always, our greatest strengths can be our worst enemy.

Wasting time is called Sabbath. It is an invitation from God to stop—really *stop*. It is a call to cease from striving. It is a practice that reminds us it is not our strength but God's strength working through us that accomplishes anything. We are utilizing, not wasting, time when we are with friends, loved ones, or alone enjoying an "unpurposeful" walk in life. Practices of rest, recreation, and restoration are gifts from God. They allow us to find a rhythm that is sustainable in a world where there will always be work to accomplish. I may never read about dragons, but I am finding ways to stop. What about you?

What can you do this week that you enjoy or you think you might enjoy?

What practices of Sabbath have you engaged in previously that work well for you?

I'M ON YOUR SIDE

WHEN I WAS IN graduate school my partner and I would commute together since his job was just two exits from my campus. It was our first year of marriage, and this helped us connect and learn a lot about one another. The mornings were usually very quiet, but the afternoon commute back home was loud. I vented. A lot. I vented about everything that had happened in class.

Occasionally during these discussions he would have to say to me, "I'm on your side."

I was stunned when I heard him say this. I didn't fully understand how or why, but I must have been communicating distrust during our conversation. We weren't fighting. I was venting about injustice in academia. Still, I kept the part about how I felt like an imposter out of our discussion. Both were true, but I was unwilling to be vulnerable with him. I kept him outside of my "wall of defense."

Don Richard Riso and Russ Hudson, in *The Wisdom of the Enneagram*, propose that we all receive unconscious messages from our parents during childhood. The unconscious childhood message for Eights is, "It's not OK to be vulnerable or trust anyone." I have a longing to know that I will not be betrayed and that my friends have my back. In these discussions with my partner, I think I wanted to hear that he saw the injustice and the way it had impacted me.

"I'm on your side" is a phrase I've heard dozens of times over the past decade from people who love me and are out for my good. Without realizing it, I can suddenly go on the defensive, feeling the need to protect myself . . . but from what?

Our lack of trust pushes those who are trying to partner with us away. Praise the Lord—no really—praise God that I have a partner who can and does speak to me directly by telling me, "I'm on your side." It is crucial that we all have people in our lives with whom we have strong trust so they can invade our space. What am I feeling internally that is building up walls? What will happen if I trust someone? What will happen if I practice vulnerability?

If individual experiences have made us distrustful of people, it's life-giving to be in relationships that allow brave reflection. Maybe we've been stomped on by people or beat up because of our social reality, and there are good reasons that we have spent much of our lives on the defensive. Maybe we've been hurt after putting trust in people who failed us. Whether it's an individual or a system that failed us, we want to move toward connection with others. We have to let people in and trust them. When we do, we can practice deepening our vulnerability with them.

Invite Jesus into the questions above and allow the words of this hymn, "'Tis So Sweet to Trust in Jesus," published by Louisa M. R. Stead in 1882, to anchor you:

'Tis so sweet to trust in Jesus,
Just to take Him at His Word
Just to rest upon His promise,
Just to know, "Thus saith the Lord!"
Jesus, Jesus, how I trust Him!
How I've proved Him o'er and o'er.
Jesus, Jesus, precious Jesus!
Oh, for grace to trust Him more!

MAMA'S NOT HAPPY WITH ME

"PATIENT" IS NOT A WORD anyone would use to describe me. I am. . . . intense. Diligent. Courageous. Intentional. Committed . . . but not patient. Sometimes when confronted with incompetence, I'm a straight-up bully.

Being a parent of two toddlers has been the single most intense test of my patience. No one is more loyal than an Eight to the people they love if they are under attack, but sometimes we are the ones attacking. Attacking with our words, our energy, and even sometimes our physical presence if we are humble enough to admit it to ourselves. One of my sons in particular triggers all my Eightness.

I distinctly remember having to walk away from a conversation with him when he had just turned three. I ran into the kitchen and yelled, "Why won't he listen? *I'm* in charge!"

My partner gently said, "He's three."

I started to laugh aloud and realized what I had said. Here I was fighting a just-turned-three-year-old. I mean I was *in* it—my entire self: body, mind, and soul. This was *my* house and he was going to know that. How asinine! How ridiculous was I being? And yet I was committed.

I wish I could say I repented (read: "changed"), turned from my wicked ways, and became the nicest mama ever. I didn't. I continued to struggle. I continue to struggle. There is something in his energy of opposition that triggers me. He seems to have exposed that "angry button," as our family therapist calls it, and is exploiting it to get a reaction out of me. I regret the way I used my volume and presence that day. I learned that as an Eight I needed to choose compassion.

For the next few weeks if I showed any sign of disappointment my son would go to his papa and say, "Mama's not happy with me."

Each time I overheard him saying that, it crushed me. I love my son. I am happy with him. It was me!

Given a few years of distance from that season in our lives, I can see what was operating in me: stress. And when an Eight gets stressed out, everyone better duck and cover, because some force is coming after you. Stress comes in the form of job transition, excessive responsibility, relational conflict, and new risk-taking.

When we find ourselves in a transition or season of stress that reveals a need for Christlikeness, we have an invitation from our loving Savior to be made into his image. This process of transformation confronts the poverty of our soul. It is important that we receive grace and mercy for ourselves and not judgment. It is important that we offer love instead of withholding it in order to protect and defend ourselves.

Take a few minutes to review your week. Has someone communicated that you are not happy with them?

Can you think of a relationship that has been affected by the way you interacted with them? Review that person's words. Is that an accurate picture of how you felt? If not, what was at play that made them feel that way?

Review the instances again and see where you can find God's presence in the picture.

THAT TIME YOU
REALIZED IT

THE MOMENT AN EIGHT realizes they have disintegrated into the dark side of a Five can be one of life's scariest. You can be going along, business as usual, and suddenly feel agitated when someone asks for a little of your time. You can have someone you love and with whom you enjoy spending time touch you and experience a visceral reaction to it. You suddenly realize that the only thing that can satisfy you is personal space and privacy. Where you once needed and wanted contact, you are now retreating.

You may even have experienced a productive workday and are able to debate a friend over a drink, but you are not available to your partner, children, or family. You can sense a desire to hoard time and space for yourself instead of living passionately toward the people you love. If you have been in this place, you are in good company.

We can tell when it's happening. Maybe we're consuming Flamin' Hot Cheetos at a rate that will destroy our intestines. Perhaps we start watching a show on Netflix and find ourselves at one a.m. still hitting "next episode." We slowly withdraw. We find it almost impossible to connect with the ones we love the most and for whom we want to be the most available.

It's interesting that we hoard our time and presence from the very people with whom we are in relationships of mutuality and love. It's the people who know our weaknesses and can offer tenderness to our frailty whom we wall up around when under stress. This is incredibly strange given that those are the human beings who offer us the health we need.

Sometimes this catches us off guard. I know it does me. Then we begin to spiral into activities that don't restore us but only numb the deep lament of anger and stress we carry. Even the sexual intensity we once loved is gone and threatens to expose us in a way that signals to our partner we are not well. It has helped in those times to name what I am feeling, to speak it to myself, a mentor, a journal, and get the words out:

"I'm hoping my husband doesn't try to initiate intimacy."

"God, please let that meeting be canceled so I can stay at home and have a drink."

"Help! Everyone wants something from me!"

When we find ourselves disintegrating or in stress, we can kindly remind ourselves that we don't have to be weighed down by the frustrations, anger, and gravity of the wrong things in our world. We can remind ourselves that God's mercies are new each day and we can be replenished and restored. We can decide to make ourselves available, starting with our Creator. Nothing is being asked of us but our presence.

What are the things that cause you to withhold yourself from your loved ones?

Say to yourself, "God will replenish me. I will not stay empty."

Take time to draw an image of what this looks like in your life. It can be a scene or just one object.

HUMILITY IS
FOR SUCKERS

MARIA WAS SINGING the song *"No Hay Lugar Mas Grande."* I looked over at her and listened: "There is no higher or greater place than at your feet. Here I'll stay, where no one can harm me. You lift me up." I ended up in tears.

I didn't mean to fall apart, but knowing Maria's story of growing up in the poverty and oppression of a border town moved me. Here she was, freely offering her melody to God with a smile on her face, and my body was aching with resentment for something that had happened that day. I was singing my harmony, but I was not free. How was she able to submit such a sincere prayer before God?

Maria knew that the radical call of discipleship leads us downward. We submit ourselves, we empty ourselves, we relinquish power and control. It is downward each step of the way. Our natural response is to reach for power and justice, but Jesus speaks against retaliation even when we have the right to seek vengeance. Jesus' radical call to discipleship offends my sensibilities—he makes me mad! This way of humility does not come easily for an Eight.

In ancient Near Eastern culture, personal vengeance was legal. An "eye for an eye" was the way of the world. You hurt me; I hurt you back. And it is still very much a part of our lives today. In fact, we often move the needle a little further—you hurt me, I hurt you worse.

But Jesus commands us not to seek vengeance when we have been harmed or strike back when we have been shamed. He calls the poor who have been ripped off to give more and those who have been forced into free labor to work harder.

We can imagine the negativity Jesus may have sensed from his hearers. He was tearing up their sense of order and speaking against their human instinct.

What are you saying, Jesus? If I experience abuse in my home, am I supposed to trust them again?

No.

If someone in my work sabotages my career, am I supposed to work on a project with them?

No.

This is not a call to put yourself or keep yourself in an experience where you are being abused or mistreated. This is a call to radical forgiveness motivated by love—our love for God and his love for us. Since resentment also impacts our health, forgiveness is also about loving ourselves. When we are mistreated and mistrusted, Jesus calls us to consider how love might compel us to offer forgiveness. When someone misunderstands us and makes life difficult, we can trust that God is aware and will intervene for us the way he always has for his people.

An inability to practice forgiveness and humility is a shared trait of Eights, but it is particularly enhanced when we come from experiences of trauma or abandonment. I have seen people say, "You are dead to me" and choose not to reconcile with a close friend who has broken trust. This is even celebrated in some of our cultures—for Latino males it is a sign of strength.

We are stubborn to admit being wrong and we never forget injuries against us. The humility to forgive as well as seek forgiveness requires a painful amount of vulnerability for an Eight.

What does a radical response of forgiveness mean for how we treat others who have mistreated us?

Ask the Holy Spirit to give you strength to embody this costly call.

STRENGTH FOR SOLIDARITY

THE GOSPEL OF LUKE was formative in my early years. It helped me believe I was joining a community that was pushing back the darkness and rebuilding a just world. I truly believed that if we lived in hospitality, solidarity, and mutuality, the church could compel people to know Christ.

But instead of a fragrant aroma of solidarity in Christ, I found a stench. A stench of complacency and complicity that lingered in the narcissism and consumerism that was called church. That odor is so potent I sometimes feel like leaving—don't you?

I hear the voice of our Creator inviting us to examine our role in the world. We are living in a moment that is ripe with invitation for us to be the people Jesus lived and died for, the community that is a testimony of the love and justice of God.

In the church we are to be the embodiment of oneness, but we live as though we are not even related. In the tension between where we are and what is supposed to be, the Eight can do one of two things: either we can give a middle finger to those in the church we don't feel are living up to our standards and disregard their humanity, or we can learn to speak truth to power in compassion and patience. Let me tell you why this is hard for me.

Not too long ago I spent a year visiting refugees at the US-Mexico border as well as visiting Central American countries hurting from natural disasters, gang violence, and sex trafficking. One day a Honduran neighbor called me, distraught. Her sister had been detained by immigration authorities, and they were planning to slap an ankle monitor on her and put her on a bus to San Antonio. I got information about the detention center and the sister's inmate number from my neighbor, and I went to see if I could intervene on this woman's behalf.

This is just one example of how proximity to pain impacts patience. Recently I was hanging out with Central American mothers in my community and talking with them about the challenges of educating our children. Being around marginalized people and hearing their stories has impacted how I see social policies and practices. Proximity makes immigration issues not merely political but personal, which makes it all the more difficult to speak the truth with patience.

As Eights we lead best through strength and stability. We have an ability to thrive under pressure and take risks. The work of equity and justice requires a willingness to enter into tough conversations. It requires truth-telling and paving a way forward. Solidarity with a Latina sister is not about holding hands and singing songs; it's about protecting her. This is done not only through compassion but through disruption as well. We Eights were created for these roles; we are natural challengers who will protect the ones we love. We will call for truth-telling wherever there is abuse of power.

What would it look like to live in true solidarity with the vulnerable?

What practices of compassion and patience can we ask the Spirit to empower us in as we do the work of truth-telling?

DO I HAVE THE
ENERGY FOR THIS?

ON MY DESK I HAVE an unopened letter from a close friend. This letter is from someone I deeply love like family. The relationship I have with this person has lasted almost two decades and has been one of the most profound ways God has shaped me.

I haven't opened the letter. I'm not sure I want to, and I don't know if this is my Eight being wise or my Five child questioning whether I can spare the energy. In the last few years this relationship has followed a pattern: attempts at reconciliation followed by disengagement. Both of us at different times have chosen to opt out of speaking because we are being triggered by the other's accusations.

Each of us has confessed at times that we don't have the bandwidth to enter into a process that we know will ultimately bring healing. As people of faith, we hold on to the command to be reconciled and the promise of restoration. As friends who both live in the gut space, it is hard for us to lean into humility. We are committed, but we have been asking with each step, "Do I have the energy for this?"

I want to speak freedom to those of us who are going through situations like this. Being a person of peace does not dictate a time frame, but it does invite a process. A desire for peace is a desire for wholeness and flourishing for all. In conversations with our therapist, spiritual director, partner, or community, we can find a way forward toward healing. If we are willing to find relationships in which we can truly be vulnerable and allow ourselves to trust, they can help us become our most authentic self. They will help us discern how long we get to stare at a letter on our desk.

Communities of trust and vulnerability are critical to becoming whole. These are the people who know our cultural nuance and tell this Latina Eight wing Seven to count to ten before engaging. These are the people who will compel the Asian Eight wing Nine not to sit with his stirring passion but to take the risk or address the conflict. Our friends don't want us to live with regret for what we did or did not do. Our community of trusted friends will be agents of healing. Without mentorship, partnership, and friendship, we may regret the decision we make about that letter.

In the end, I'm not sure what will happen to this friendship. I get angry. I feel accused. As a Latina who experiences social marginalization I think it's unfair for my friend to ask me to empty more. The injustice of it all fumes me. The arrogance I see triggers me. The brokenness I intuit invites me. My pride justifies me. And my Creator compels me to find a way toward peace.

Do you have relationships in your life that need a new way forward? How is your Creator inviting you to be a person of peace and wholeness?

CLOUD OF WITNESSES

LIVING AS AN EIGHT can wear us down. Instability and violence will always exist in our world as a result of fear and abuse of power. Keeping sacred rhythms that lead to belief in God's goodness will help us survive.

There are many white contemplatives, such as Thomas Merton, Richard Rohr, Ruth Haley Barton, and Robert Mulholland, who have informed me in this area, but sacred rhythms are also modeled to us by women of color—by our *abuelitas*, our black aunties, our Korean mothers, and our Egyptian sisters. The ability to trust God in the midst of chaos and bring our unbelief and pain to God's throne are the practices of the church on the margins. Women on the margins even model this in the biblical narrative. Consider the woman who wept at Jesus' feet and the women at the tomb who wrapped his corpse while they agonized about what Jesus had promised.

As we reflect on the faith handed down from our *abuelas*, *halmeonis*, and grannies, we are reminded that we are a part of a narrative that is beyond us. We remember singing in church with them, even if we made fun of the songs because we wanted something more modern. We have flashbacks to our Holy Communion or confirmation and remember that our aunties were so happy we were making the family proud. We recall gatherings of prayer and storytelling in which we heard how God brought them through suffering. Those of us raised in collective cultures typically see ourselves in light of those who have come before us. What we know and who we have become are a result of our ancestors. That is why we honor them, not to worship them but to tell our story.

The faith of our ancestors, the written testimony of our faith, and the current cloud of global witnesses will serve as a guide when our gut reaction leaves us hyperventilating from the reality of life. This triad of witness is what I imagine in this Scripture from Hebrews:

Therefore, since we are surrounded by such a great cloud of witnesses, let us throw off everything that hinders and the sin that so easily entangles. And let us run with perseverance the race marked out for us, fixing our eyes on Jesus, the pioneer and perfecter of faith. For the joy set before him he endured the cross, scorning its shame, and sat down at the right hand of the throne of God. Consider him who endured such opposition from sinners, so that you will not grow weary and lose heart. (Hebrews 12:1-3)

Injustice and poverty will always be with us. Therefore healthy prophets, grounded leaders, and whole followers of Jesus will be central to the revolution of God's love, justice, and goodness for the world. When we feel our chest tightening, let's remember that we are not alone.

What rhythms were passed on to you from a family member or mentor? How might you commit to practicing them this week?

Draw a picture or a name collage of your cloud of witnesses. Include people from your community who have laid spiritual foundations for you, biblical characters who are important to you, and people currently in your life both locally and globally who encourage rhythms and practices of sustainability.

TIME-INS

WHEN GOD INVITES US to disconnect from something, someone, or someplace that is unhealthy for us, it is not so much a time-out as much as it is a time-in.

Parenting research is helping us to understand that a time-out isolates the child from the relationship, and ignoring or sidelining the child can actually cause more harm than good. The better solution is a time-in, where you quietly invite your struggling child to sit near you and talk about their emotions and allow them to slowly calm down. As a parent I struggle with that, because it affects my time. I know, I'm selfish—but I'm honest.

However, I can completely understand the logic, especially when it comes to children who have experienced some form of trauma. We ourselves have been children, and in a very real way we remain children of the God who is our Creator and sustainer.

Giving ourselves a time-in allows us to be in God's presence but away from the people or patterns that are damaging us. A rule of life—or patterns of spiritual discipline that we build our daily routine around—allows us space for contemplation, which is necessary for the health of an Eight in times of stress.

One of the most meaningful accounts of a time-in with God is the story of Moses in Exodus 2. Here is a man who has experienced immense childhood trauma: he was fostered in the home of Pharaoh, raised by his Jewish mother and sister, exposed to Egyptian schooling and rites of passage, and aware that he was one of only a few Jewish boys who survived the genocide committed by the people who were now fostering him. We know enough about fostering and adoption-related mental health issues, as well as those related to surviving violence, to realize that Moses had a lot to process.

When he reached adulthood, Moses witnessed the suffering of his own people in slavery. And one day, seeing the mistreatment of a Jewish brother by an Egyptian overseer, he snapped! With all of that rage and anger flooding his being, he took matters into his own hands and killed the Egyptian barehanded. Afraid that Pharaoh would have him killed for murdering an Egyptian, he fled to Midian, where he stayed for forty years.

That time in voluntary exile was an extended time-in with God. Moses slowed down and disconnected from the center of power. He went from being a high-ranking person in the family of Pharaoh to being a hard-working, average-Joe shepherd with a lot more time for contemplation. Moses had time to reflect on his childhood with his mother and sister. He also had time to reflect on his time in the palace as a teen and young man, sitting in luxury while the empire that fed him oppressed his community, including his relatives. He carried with him two cultures, two locations, and now he added a third, as he likely spent twice as much time in Midian as he did in Egypt.

As a Latina woman who has grown up in a bicultural world and navigated not only ethnic differences but also has a passion to liberate my community from systems of oppression that make them vulnerable to trafficking, dehumanization, and violence, I have made some terrible choices from my gut. I have never been physically violent, but I have been lethal with my words. My love for God and God's command to love my neighbor, my vision for the world as a place where God's flourishing reigns, and the reality of racial and economic injustice in the church are a recipe for a Moses moment.

In one such moment I was quick to move and slow to think, which ended in major conflict and a three-month leave of absence. In those months I met with a spiritual director, and this is what led me to the Enneagram. I reflected on what had happened that caused me to snap. I came back from my time-in and, eventually, relationships were restored and I was transformed. That experience and this story in Exodus 2 have been the most significant leadership lessons in my life.

Make space to think about how time-ins can work for you. Who can help you along? Take time to thank God for God's presence with you while you are being restored.

WEANING

WHEN CHILDREN ARE in their mother's lap with their face in her chest, they are happy. In many cultural contexts mothers cover themselves when they breastfeed. We even use words like "nursing" so we don't have to say the word "breast." But in so doing we miss out on the miracle and creativity of the breast's design.

When babies are born they can't see, yet they can wiggle their way to find food because the glands on the nipple smell like the mother's amniotic fluid. The smell helps baby recognize mama and find the milk. It's amazing! There is a biological GPS woven into our system by the Creator who helps us survive. In the arms of a mother a child finds nourishment, comfort, and rest.

The image given to us in Psalm 131 asks us to consider another invitation given by God. It is an image that can be found in any generation, any culture, any socioeconomic situation. It is a feminine image of the divine that invites us to see God as mother—as breastfeeding mother. God is the one who has given the psalmist nourishment, comfort, and rest. It is an image of connectedness and dependency, of intimacy and vulnerability.

> My heart is not proud, LORD,
>   my eyes are not haughty;
> I do not concern myself with great matters
>   or things too wonderful for me.
> But I have calmed and quieted myself;
>   I am like a weaned child with its mother,
>   like a weaned child I am content.
>
> Israel, put your hope in the LORD
>   both now and forevermore. (Psalm 131:1-3)

This powerful image of vulnerability invites us as Eights to consider not needing to be so strong. We need not concern ourselves with things beyond our limitations. We need to acknowledge that we *have* limitations and invite ourselves to stillness. We can pause from producing or protecting, which is incredibly hard when the world needs us to be powerful.

A child who is weaned has transitioned into a deeper form of love and trust. Spiritually, this happens after a season of denial of the milk that so nourished and satisfied us. It causes us to rest in God's love and provision in a way we have never experienced or even knew existed. It is a season that comes after wrestling. Wrestling with what we know in our spiritual journey with God. Wrestling for what we want from life.

The process of physical weaning causes anxiety and anger toward the mother. The baby thinks she wants the milk, but what she really desires is comfort and satisfaction. By then the baby is eating delicious food—in Near Eastern culture, like many cultures around the world today, the child is weaned around three years of age. There are teeth and words, and the child asks for a lot of solid food. So breast-feeding is not about the milk—the baby wants comfort.

"I have quieted myself"—in other words, I have stopped complaining. I have stopped asking for something I don't really need or want anyway. This image is of a child lying on her mother, clinging to her breasts not for milk but for safety and intimacy. The feel is familiar and the smell is home. The psalm invites us to this type of rest with God our mother. It is a place of maturity where we can let go of what we once thought we needed or who we once thought we were.

This invitation has been important to me as an Eight. I am often expected to provide nurture and safety for many around me. Quieting my soul is not something I am good at, and allowing myself to relax in the arms of God and not go back to the things I knew before is hard. When we find ourselves in the lap of our mother God, we offer up a prayer for indifference (not my will), a prayer for wisdom, a prayer of quiet trust without judgment. And we end with a prayer of vulnerable petition, making our true needs and desires known to God.

> Make a pile of blankets or pillows in a comfortable corner in the shape of a small nest. If that feels weird, go to the chair you like to chill in. Rest there for twenty minutes. This is your spiritual act of worship.

WAITING SUCKS

WE HAVE SOLUTIONS, we have the drive, and we are pretty sure we can make things happen. To wait is to give up control. And to give up control is to be weak—or so we think.

When we consider the injustices that affect our communities—the deaths of black bodies, the attacks on black dignity, and the lack of police accountability—they all make clear a widespread acceptance of systems of racism. The Covid-19 pandemic disproportionately affected vulnerable communities both from a health and socioeconomic perspective all over the world, yet people fought the usage of masks. Children were separated from parents and refugee families suffered under our watch as we hoped for policies to change.

Even though it sucks, we wait! Waiting involves expectation and longing. Waiting is active, not passive, as it works toward something. Waiting implies hope in the midst of suffering.

While I don't know anyone who is good at waiting, we Eights have to be particularly attentive to how our impatience affects others. We set the pace, and we expect people to follow. If we are not careful, our actions can create an environment that is destructive to our families and our communities. We want to move faster than our friends—and God.

What else can we do but wait on God's good promise of justice and deliverance? God made a promise to break the oppression of God's people not through violence, not through power or might, but through a brown Palestinian boy born to a young virgin into a refugee family during a violent regime. And from this humble place, the liberator would reign with mercy and justice.

But that was after four hundred years of silence. So we are in good company with God's people who have waited over the centuries. Abraham and Sarah waited to have the child God promised, and even though they committed acts of injustice and carelessness in the meantime, God in grace fulfilled the promise. The Israelites waited to enter the Promised Land and waited for return from exile, and even though they failed in many ways, God in grace fulfilled the promise. We, too, in our broken and brilliant humanity, wait for Jesus to bring complete renewal and healing to a hurting world, and we too will see glimpses of God's grace.

We know Christ has come, and we long for him to return to restore order to the world—*and* we expect him to come in the present! Let's practice expectant waiting and preparation for the coming of Christ. Let's invite longing and hoping. In the meantime, we can acknowledge that waiting sucks!

Read Psalm 27:13-14:

> I remain confident of this:
>> I will see the goodness of the LORD
>> in the land of the living.
> Wait for the LORD;
>> be strong and take heart
>> and wait for the LORD.

Name your longings to God and write down both what those longing are and how you will participate in seeing those promises fulfilled.

HELP TO LISTEN

STAYING STILL.

Lying down.

Quieting yourself.

These are the names of classes that Eights would fail.

We oftentimes need others to remind us to listen. And there are very few people in our lives as Eights who will do this—who will let us know that our pace and our intensity need to decrease. When we do find those people, we need to keep them close, because their whispers will help us retain our balance in life.

I know I was thankful for a recent interaction in which a friend gently redirected me. I was expressing a desire for us to process the uprisings happening in Black and Brown communities, and I went deep into the issues on many levels.

My friend's reply was simply, "That's a lot to process."

I think this was his way of asking for me not to add any more information to the conversation and to allow space for quiet and listening. Right as he made his statement, the image of Eli and Samuel came to mind from 1 Samuel 3.

In this passage the boy Samuel hears a voice calling out to him in the middle of the night, and it wakes him up repeatedly. He mistakes it for Eli, the high priest and the second-to-last Israelite judge. He continues to ask Eli what he wants, and then finally Eli realizes the Lord is calling Samuel. Eli tells him, "Go and lie down, and if he calls you, say, 'Speak, Lord, for your servant is listening.'"

Samuel laid down and the Lord came and stood near him and called his name again. Then Samuel said, "Speak, for your servant is listening."

Eli helped Samuel adopt a posture of listening, even if the news that came to Samuel was bad news for Eli. We need people in our lives who will help us do the same. These people don't have to be perfect, but they do have to take seriously the disciplines of silence and listening prayer. They should be people who prioritize and worship God. They are the ones who will get us to pay attention when God is trying to guide us toward a better way to live. They will invite us to the counterintuitive practices of quieting ourselves enough to hear God's guidance.

Listening requires silence. Silence reminds us we are on a journey. In those moments we are able to see the length of the journey and pay attention to patterns. Silence also gives us the space to notice the passion within us; it allows us to be connected and attentive to the source of our life. Silence instructs us how to speak by helping us discern what we are supposed to hear and what we are supposed to say. Silence requires strength, but only in silence can we slow ourselves down enough to truly hear.

What makes it hard for you to discern when it is God's voice speaking? Who around you can guide you to a place of listening? Get help getting to stillness. Invite God to speak.

SUCKING AIR

EIGHTS HAVE INCREDIBLE passion and power. We have the ability to change the mood in a room. When we hear this, we are not sure whether to laugh or cry, depending on how it last played out. Our influence and power can be used to inspire and connect. It can also be used to manipulate or dominate. We can take up "space" in the room and demand either verbally or otherwise that people do as we say.

I work with a lot of Eights because we are leaders who are working collectively to innovate and challenge the status quo in our institutions. It's always easier to see the way others wield their power than it is to reflect on our own. Think about how you've seen this happen. I've watched leaders enter a room and with their presence, facial expression, and volume suck all of the energy from it.

I have witnessed many Eights, males especially, walk into a room as if nothing could have possibly started before they arrived. The door swings open, they start talking (usually in a volume much louder than anyone else is using), and say something like, "OK, let's get this meeting started. I'd like to get out of here as quickly as possible—I have things to do."

People in the room comply, especially if their cultural norms are more hierarchical. It doesn't mean they enjoy it.

As Eights we may have no idea how someone has been impacted by our directness. Our team members may feel overpowered, shut down, or manipulated by us. If we are more verbal, we can often talk our way to convincing others they are wrong. I've heard Eights say to their teams, "I need to know who's with me. Because if you can't get on board I need to know."

When confronted by those who recognize that our directness is doing damage, we will likely deflect and defend ourselves—only to later confess to a trusted friend that we may have come on too strong. We are unlikely to apologize for it, but we might try to not repeat it. I have been told that Eights are exhausting and exhausted in these situations.

Our experience as Eights will vary as men and women and depending on our cultural values. It would be perfectly normal for a woman of color to be skeptical if someone with social and racial power forcefully disagreed with us. We might either internalize with a lot of self-doubt (which is atypical for a male Eight) or fiercely attack the mansplaining. Either way, we don't usually gain much from the exchange.

In those cases we need spiritual discernment and community to help us sort through whether we are disintegrating or experiencing injustice. The invitation for us is to live into our grounded true self. We want to operate from a place of strength, not intimidation. We also want to acknowledge that if we are from marginalized communities, we are free to stand against oppression.

What is God stirring in you as you read these examples? What interactions are you revisiting? What spaces have you been in where you've witnessed collateral damage? How can you live into strength without charging ahead and harming others?

WE WILL NOT FEAR

COURAGE IS ABOUT acknowledging a bigger purpose and a bigger power.

My understanding of courage came from my mother. She had the courage to move to a new country and reestablish herself. To learn to speak a new language and take on new customs. She had to learn not only to survive but to thrive.

My mother embodied courage. She taught me that no one could ever steal your dream. She taught me that when you fall, you get back up. She taught me that no matter how poor or rich, everyone is valuable to God, and the more voices are heard, the better we can all be together. Watching her name and confess her fears while maintaining faith, *mi mama Colombiana* displayed and taught me about courage.

When we Eights live courageously, we accept the beauty and fierceness God has given us as a way to model that to our communities. We teach them that courage is not merely an action but a way to live.

The words of Scripture tell us we can operate in courage! Why? Because the Lord is with us. God will never abandon, desert, leave, quit, give up on, reject, discard, or forsake us.

God won't turn his back on us. Our courage comes from the knowledge that we are not alone.

This is repeated in many places in Scripture, including Psalm 46:

> God is our refuge and strength,
> an ever-present help in trouble.
> Therefore we will not fear.
> The LORD Almighty is with us;
> the God of Jacob is our fortress.
> (Psalm 46:1-2, 11)

Take time to reflect on the words of Psalm 46. Write down the words "fear" and "courage" and make a list under each of what comes to mind.

Name your fears. Acknowledge them. Write them in a journal. Say them aloud as you take a walk.

Confess those fears to a trusted friend. When we speak our fears aloud, they lose their power. And sometimes hearing ourselves say them gives us perspective.

Stand firm in your faith—pray Scriptures or sing a song over yourself so you can hear truth. "Be strong and courageous. Do not be afraid; do not be discouraged, for the LORD your God will be with you wherever you go" (Joshua 1:9).

Name it; confess it; stand firm!

HOPE THROUGH LAMENT

HOPE IS LIVING in light of God's goodness in the midst of God's silence. The silence of God could not have been more potent than in the hundreds of years between the promise of a Messiah to God's people in the Old Testament and the birth of Jesus. Those who were still engaged in practices of worship and witness of God's love and justice had to dig deep and believe through many generations without much of God's promised presence.

Zechariah and his wife, Elizabeth, were people of prayer and faithfulness yet they did not have a son. In Near Eastern culture, infertility brought shame on one's family. Zechariah's prayers rose with the incense he was burning in the temple as he fulfilled his priestly duties (Luke 1:8-9). These were prayers of lament, prayers of anguish, and prayers of hope. He and his wife longed to have family and honor in the community. God was inviting Zechariah to allow the scent and smoke of the incense to fill his eyes and nose as the cries of his prayers filled his own ears. He prayed, wrestled, and waited in hope.

Then, the angel of the Lord was there, saying, "Your prayer has been heard" (Luke 1:13).

Ugandan scholar Emmanuel Kataongole, in his book *Born from Lament,* argues this: "In the midst of suffering, hope takes the form of arguing and wrestling with God. If we understand it as lament, such arguing and wrestling is not merely a sentiment, not merely a cry of pain. It is a way of mourning, of protesting to, appealing to, and engaging God."

As Eights we lament. Sometimes people think we are too pessimistic or too hard on people, but we just can't settle for the status quo. We are going to yell and cry and sometimes cuss in our prayers and spiritual conversations with others. Not only do we have the freedom to protest; we free others to be honest with themselves and God as well. We are not going to stand for an expression of faith that diminishes how much evil impacts the world, and we are not planning on being overcome by this evil. Eights will fight for hope and joy in a beautifully assertive way.

Brothers and sisters in the majority world, or Global South, live in contexts that encourage public expressions of grief. Corporate lament is acceptable because they understand that it elevates the reality of our collective humanity. It invites those of us who don't wait well to wait in hope for our own longings. It also invites us to wait in hope for the rescue of a broken world where many suffer under injustice.

What lament have you not let out? What release is your soul asking for this day?

If you have some incense at your disposal, bring it out. Use your arms to follow the smoke as it rises up with your prayers. Freely long in God's presence.

MY PRAISES RISE

I LOVE MY FAMILY, but sometimes the first thing that comes out of my mouth when I see them is a harsh or critical statement. Under that negativity is a deep well of mixed thoughts, both positive and negative, but what surfaces is my gut reaction to the first thing I see.

Many times it's something I have no control over, like walking into a room where all the toys have been taken out. I even used to try to stay in bed in the morning until I was awake enough to come up with two positive things to say—this was a discipline to show love to my family full of Sevens and Ones.

Gratitude and praise lie deep in the heart of an Eight, but sometimes it's difficult to get them out into the open. Offering gratitude to God and practicing radical self-love are important, for as Eights our journey is filled with both opposition and adventure.

Thank you, God, for making us strong and independent. Thank you for the courage to speak truth to power. Thank you for the willingness to take risks to disrupt and challenge things that need to change. Thank you for the passion to get all we can out of life. Thank you for empowering us to protect those we love. Thank you for the faith to believe in a better world. Thank you for the resilience to pursue this dream.

The practice of praise in relationship to others and God disciplines us to be for something rather than against. It invites us to soften so we can tell the ones we love, including our Creator, that we are thankful. We praise God for all that God is to us and all that has been done for us. We lift up our voice, even offer our hands up in exaltation and surrender as a way of communicating to God that we see reality. God is good and God intends good for God's creation.

We worship God not because the circumstances of our lives are full of flourishing. We worship God not because we are free from the impact of pain and sorrow. We worship God not because we feel excited about the hard things we endure. We worship God because somehow in the midst of those circumstances God is present with us.

In the Bible, those who follow Jesus and love God are enabled by the Spirit to worship God at all times. In the good times and the hard times they gather collectively to worship God.

As a woman of color, I look to those in my community and within my ethnic tradition who have led the way in offering worship to God. I look to the worship practices of my ancestors who endured conditions no human being should ever have to face. I look to the praise from the *abuelas* who held the household together and taught us the ways of God. I look to the prayers of the mothers who continue to teach me to lift up a shout even when life is unjust and painful. I look to the friends who write melodies and lyrics that remind me God's presence and promises require praise regardless of circumstance and feelings.

The words below were penned by Edwin Santiago, whose friendship has been a model to me of worship in all seasons; he wrote this song specially as a way to help himself through a difficult time. This song, "Mi Alabanza Seguirá," has been sung by young people all over the world in a language that is not their own, but the invitation remains as potent as ever.

Read these words below and make space to name the good and the bad.

Aleluya aleluya	Hallelujah, hallelujah
Mi alabanza sube a ti	My praises rise to you
En las buenas y las malas	In the good and bad
Mi alabanza seguirá.	My praise will continue.

Make space to tell God of God's goodness with your praise. As the psalmist says,

> **May these words of my mouth and this meditation of my heart**
> **be pleasing in your sight,**
> **LORD, my Rock and my Redeemer.**
> **(Psalm 19:14)**

ENNEAGRAM
DAILY REFLECTIONS

SUZANNE STABILE,
SERIES EDITOR